TABLE OF CONTENTS

BRAZIL TRAVEL GUIDE

2024

Insider Tips for Exploring Rio, Sao Paulo, Carnaval And Beyond

Mark Sims

"Ah, Brazil! The mere mention of the name conjures up images of vibrant colors, infectious rhythms, and warm, golden sand. A land of breathtaking beauty, rich cultural heritage, and passionate people, Brazil is a destination that will leave you enchanted, inspired, and maybe even a little bit changed.

As you embark on this journey, you'll discover a country that's both modern and traditional, where ancient customs blend seamlessly with contemporary flair. You'll experience the warmth of the Brazilian people, who welcome visitors with open arms and a smile that can light up a room. You'll taste the flavors of a cuisine that's both exotic and familiar, with African, European, and indigenous influences that will tantalize your taste buds.

From the stunning beaches of Rio to the majestic Amazon rainforest, and from the Afro-Brazilian rhythms of Salvador to the modern metropolis of São Paulo, Brazil is a country that's full of surprises. And in this travel guide, we'll take you on a journey through the best of it, sharing insider tips, local secrets, and unforgettable experiences that will make your trip truly unforgettable.

So come along, and let's explore the beauty, passion, and joy of Brazil together! Get ready to fall in love with this incredible country, and to create memories that will last a lifetime."

Introduction

Why Visit Brazil?

Brazil is a place where every corner feels alive with color, rhythm, and warmth—a true haven for travelers. What makes Brazil so special is its unique blend of cultures. Indigenous, African, and European influences come together to create a vibrant tapestry of music, dance, art, and food. Here, visitors can't help but get swept up in the lively beats of samba and bossa nova, stroll through the colorful streets of Salvador, or lose themselves in the magic of Carnival, where the entire country seems to move to one joyful rhythm.

The landscapes of Brazil are just as captivating as its culture. The mighty Amazon rainforest, stretching as far as the eye can see, feels almost otherworldly in its beauty. Then there's Rio de Janeiro, where the golden sands of Copacabana meet the deep blue of the Atlantic, with the iconic Christ the Redeemer looking over it all. Whether you're hiking through the lush Tijuca Forest, marveling at the towering sand dunes of Lençóis Maranhenses, or soaking up the sun on one of Rio's famous beaches, Brazil's natural beauty feels boundless.

Its cities, too, are a perfect mix of old and new. In Rio de Janeiro, São Paulo, and Salvador, you'll find modern skyscrapers sitting alongside colonial architecture, with the buzz of the city softened by moments of tradition and history. Whether you're admiring the breathtaking views from Christ the Redeemer, climbing the colorful steps of Escadaria Selarón, or indulging in local dishes that blend a world of flavors, each city offers its own unique flavor of Brazil.

But perhaps what sets Brazil apart most is the warmth of its people. Brazilians are known for their open-hearted nature, their love for life, and their infectious sense of joy. From the moment you arrive, you're made to feel like you belong. Whether sharing a meal, dancing in the streets, or simply striking up a conversation, you'll feel the deep sense of community that Brazilians are so proud of.

Brazil is a place that doesn't just show you its beauty—it invites you in. It's a country where you'll make memories that last long after you leave, where the laughter, the music, and the warmth stay with you. And when it's time to go, you'll already be dreaming of coming back, because once you've experienced Brazil, you're forever a part of it.

History and Culture

The earliest inhabitants of Brazil were the indigenous peoples, who arrived over 10,000 years ago. These native communities developed complex societies, with their own languages, customs, and traditions. Unfortunately, the arrival of European colonizers in the 16th century had a profound impact on these communities, leading to significant loss and disruption.

The Portuguese established the first permanent settlement in 1532, and Brazil became a Portuguese colony. African slaves were brought to the country to work on sugar plantations, and their influence on Brazilian culture is still evident today. The rhythms of samba and bossa nova, the movements of capoeira, and the flavors of feijoada and acarajé all reflect the African heritage.

As Brazil grew and prospered, immigrants arrived from Europe, Asia, and the Middle East, bringing their own traditions and customs. This diversity has created a unique cultural landscape, with vibrant cities, stunning natural beauty, and a warm and welcoming people.

Brazil's history has been marked by moments of great struggle and triumph. The country fought for independence from Portugal in 1822 and navigated the challenges of building a new nation. Brazil has faced periods of dictatorship and political turmoil but has always emerged stronger and more resilient.

Today, Brazil is a thriving democracy, proud of its cultural heritage and its place in the world. Visitors can experience this warmth and hospitality firsthand, from the stunning beaches of Rio and the vibrant streets of Salvador to the breathtaking natural beauty of the Amazon and Iguazu Falls.

Brazil's cultural heritage is a treasure trove of music, dance, art, and literature. The country is home to world-renowned artists, writers, and musicians, and its festivals and celebrations are legendary. Carnaval, the Festa do Divino Espírito Santo, and the Festa de Iemanjá are just a few examples of the vibrant cultural events that take place throughout the year.

As you explore Brazil, you'll discover a nation that is proud of its history, passionate about its culture, and warm in its hospitality. We invite you to experience the beauty and wonder of Brazil, to immerse yourself in our vibrant culture, and to create unforgettable memories.

Geography and Climate

Geography

Brazil is the largest country in both South America and the Latin American region, covering an area of approximately 8.5 million square kilometers. Its vast territory encompasses a wide range of ecosystems, including the Amazon rainforest, the Pantanal wetlands, and the Atlantic Forest.

The Amazon rainforest, the world's largest tropical forest, covers over 60% of Brazil's territory. This incredible ecosystem is home to an estimated 10% of all known plant and animal species, including monkeys, macaws, and anacondas.

In contrast, the Northeast region is characterized by a semi-arid climate, with rugged landscapes and picturesque beaches. The famous Lençóis Maranhenses National Park, with its towering sand dunes and crystal-clear lagoons, is a must-visit destination.

Climate

Brazil's climate varies greatly depending on the region. The Amazon rainforest is hot and humid, with average temperatures ranging from 20°C to 30°C (68°F to 86°F). The Northeast region is generally dry, with mild winters and hot summers.

The South and Southeast regions have a more temperate climate, with mild winters and hot summers. The famous beaches of Rio de Janeiro and São Paulo are perfect for sunbathing and swimming.

Weather Patterns

Brazil is affected by various weather patterns, including the Intertropical Convergence Zone (ITCZ), which brings heavy rainfall to the Amazon region. The country is also susceptible to droughts, particularly in the Northeast.

Natural Resources

Brazil is rich in natural resources, including iron ore, copper, gold, and oil. The country is also home to an abundance of freshwater, with the Amazon River being the largest river in the world by discharge volume.

Environmental Concerns

Brazil faces various environmental challenges, including deforestation, habitat loss, and climate change. Efforts are being made to protect the Amazon rainforest and other ecosystems, but more needs to be done to preserve the country's natural heritage.

Lastly, Brazil's geography and climate are as diverse as its culture and people. From the Amazon rainforest to the sun-kissed beaches of the Northeast, this incredible country has something to offer every kind of traveler. As you explore Brazil, remember to respect and protect its natural resources, so that future generations can enjoy its beauty and wonder.

Regions of Brazil

The North Region, a land of untamed beauty, is home to the majestic Amazon rainforest, teeming with exotic wildlife and indigenous communities. Here, the mighty Amazon River flows, offering breathtaking boat tours and unforgettable encounters with pink dolphins and playful monkeys. Visit Manaus, a city nestled in the heart of the Amazon, and discover its stunning opera house, vibrant cultural scene, and mouth-watering cuisine.

In the Northeast Region, the sun-kissed beaches beckon, with crystal-clear waters and powdery white sand. Salvador, a city steeped in Afro-Brazilian culture, pulsates with vibrant rhythms, stunning colonial architecture, and mouth-watering street food. Nearby, Recife, a city with a rich history, boasts beautiful beaches, a vibrant cultural scene, and a historic center that whispers tales of the past.

In the Central-West Region, the nation's capital, Brasília, shines bright, with modernist architecture, cultural attractions, and a nightlife that never sleeps. Nearby, Cuiabá, a city surrounded by stunning natural beauty, offers wildlife spotting opportunities, indigenous cultures, and breathtaking scenery. And then there's the Pantanal, a UNESCO World Heritage Site, where caimans, toucans, and anacondas roam free.

The Southeast Region, the economic hub, throbs with energy, from Rio de Janeiro's iconic Carnival celebrations to São Paulo's world-class restaurants and cultural attractions. Ouro Preto, a historic town, boasts stunning colonial architecture, rich cultural heritage, and a charm that will leave you spellbound.

In the South Region, European influences abound, with Curitiba's innovative urban planning, Florianópolis's beautiful beaches, and Porto Alegre's rich cultural heritage. Here, the cuisine is a delicious blend of Italian, German, and Portuguese flavors, and the scenery is a feast for the eyes, with rolling hills, sparkling lakes, and picturesque villages.

Chapter 1: Planning Your Trip

When to Visit Brazil

The best time to experience the vibrant culture and stunning beauty of this incredible country is during the spring (September to November) and autumn (March to May). These periods offer mild temperatures, minimal rainfall, and a plethora of exciting festivals and events.

Summer (December to February) is peak tourist season, with warm weather and school vacations, making it ideal for beachgoers and families. However, it's also the busiest time, with higher prices and larger crowds.

Winter (June to August) is the low season, with cooler temperatures and fewer tourists, making it a great time for budget travelers and those seeking a more relaxed atmosphere.

Carnival, the world-famous celebration, takes place in February or March, with vibrant parades, music, and dancing. The Amazon rainforest is best visited during the dry season (June to November), while the Pantanal wetlands are ideal during the wet season (March to May).

Recent events and festivals include:

1. The 2024 Carnival celebrations, expected to be even more spectacular than before
2. The Amazon Rainforest Festival, promoting sustainability and indigenous cultures
3. The Pantanal Jazz Festival, featuring live music and stunning natural beauty

Remember to plan ahead, book accommodations and flights early, and research any travel requirements, such as visas or vaccinations, to ensure a smooth and unforgettable journey.

Travel Documents and Visas

As you prepare for your dream trip to Brazil, the land of vibrant culture, stunning beaches, and breathtaking landscapes, it's essential to ensure you have the right travel documents and visas. Think of these documents as the keys to unlocking the doors to an unforgettable adventure.

Passport:

Your passport is the most critical document for international travel. When visiting Brazil, make sure your passport meets the following criteria:

1. Validity: Your passport must be valid for at least six months beyond your planned departure date from Brazil. Don't risk being denied entry due to an expired passport!
2. Blank Pages: Ensure your passport has at least two blank pages for entry and exit stamps. You wouldn't want to run out of space for those precious stamps!

Visa Requirements:

Depending on your nationality, you may need a visa to enter Brazil. Think of a visa as a special permission slip to enter the country. Check the official government website or consult with the Brazilian embassy or consulate in your home country to determine the specific requirements.

1. Tourist Visa: Typically valid for 90 days, this visa can be extended for an additional 90 days. Perfect for a short trip or a longer stay!

2. Electronic Visa: Available for citizens of eligible countries, this visa is processed online and usually takes 4-5 business days to issue. Quick and convenient!

3. Visa-Free Travel: Some nationalities are eligible for visa-free travel, but be sure to check the latest requirements. A nice perk for some travelers!

Recent Updates:

Brazil has introduced some exciting updates to make travel easier:

1. Visa Waiver Program: Brazil has introduced a visa waiver program for citizens of the United States, Canada, Australia, and Japan, allowing visa-free travel for up to 90 days. A fantastic opportunity for citizens of these countries!

2. Electronic Visa Expansion: The electronic visa system has been expanded to include more nationalities, making the application process faster and more convenient. Technology at its best!

Additional Documents:

- Return Ticket or Proof of Onward Travel: You may be asked to show a return ticket or proof of onward travel when entering Brazil. Be prepared!

1. Travel Insurance: While not mandatory, travel insurance that covers medical and hospital expenses is highly recommended. Better safe than sorry!

2. Proof of Sufficient Funds: You may be asked to show proof of sufficient funds for your stay in Brazil. Be prepared to show some cash!

Tips and Reminders:

1. Make photocopies of your important documents and leave a copy with a trusted friend or family member back home. Safety first!

2. Check the official government website or consult with the Brazilian embassy or consulate for the most up-to-date information on travel documents and visas. Stay informed!

3. Apply for your visa well in advance of your trip to avoid any delays or complications. Plan ahead!

Vaccinations and Health

Vaccinations and health precautions are crucial to ensuring a safe and enjoyable journey.

Before embarking on your trip, consult your doctor or a travel clinic to discuss the necessary vaccinations and medications. Brazil requires some vaccinations, while others are recommended.

Required Vaccinations:

- Yellow Fever Vaccine: Mandatory for travelers visiting certain areas in Brazil, such as the Amazon rainforest.

Recommended Vaccinations:

- Hepatitis A and B: Protects against liver diseases.
- Typhoid: Recommended for most travelers, especially those who plan to eat or drink outside of major restaurants and hotels.
- Rabies: Recommended for travelers who plan to spend time outdoors, such as hikers or adventure seekers.

Additional Health Precautions:

1. Malaria: Take antimalarial medication if traveling to high-risk areas.
2. Dengue Fever: Prevent mosquito bites by using insect repellents and wearing protective clothing.
3. Zika Virus: Take precautions against mosquito bites, especially for pregnant women.

Tips and Reminders:

1. Consult your doctor or travel clinic at least 4-6 weeks before your trip to ensure timely vaccinations.
2. Pack a travel health kit with essentials like insect repellents, sunscreen, and pain relievers.
3. Stay hydrated and bring a refillable water bottle.
4. Avoid eating undercooked meat or raw vegetables.
5. Practice good hygiene and wash your hands frequently.

By prioritizing your health and taking the necessary precautions, you'll be free to enjoy the vibrant culture, stunning beaches, and breathtaking landscapes of Brazil.

Travel Insurance

As the travel industry continues to evolve, travel insurance has become an essential component of trip planning. In 2024, governments and travel providers are mandating travel insurance requirements to ensure tourists are adequately protected against unforeseen medical and travel-related expenses.

Why Travel Insurance is Essential for Brazil

1. Medical Expenses: Brazil's public healthcare system is generally good, but private hospitals and medical facilities may require upfront payment for services. Travel insurance ensures you're covered for medical expenses, including hospital stays, surgeries, and evacuations.

2. Trip Cancellations or Interruptions: Flight delays, natural disasters, or personal emergencies can force you to cancel or interrupt your trip. Travel insurance reimburses you for non-refundable expenses, such as flights, accommodations, and tour bookings.

3. Travel Delays: Flight delays or lost luggage can cause inconvenience and additional expenses. Travel insurance provides compensation for delays, lost or stolen luggage, and travel-related expenses.

4. Adventure Activities: Brazil offers a range of adventure activities like hiking, surfing, and paragliding. Travel insurance covers accidents or injuries sustained during these activities.

Key Features to Look for in Travel Insurance for Brazil

1. Medical Coverage: Ensure the policy covers medical expenses, including hospital stays, surgeries, and evacuations.

2. Trip Cancellation or Interruption: Choose a policy that reimburses non-refundable expenses due to trip cancellations or interruptions.

3. Travel Delays: Opt for a policy that compensates for delays, lost or stolen luggage, and travel-related expenses.

4. Adventure Activities: If you plan to engage in adventure activities, ensure the policy covers accidents or injuries sustained during these activities.

5. Policy Limits: Check the policy limits for medical expenses, trip cancellations, and travel delays.

6. Deductible: Understand the deductible amount and how it applies to claims.

7. Pre-Existing Conditions: Disclose any pre-existing medical conditions and understand how they affect coverage.

Recent Updates:

- Travel Restrictions: Understand how travel restrictions affect coverage and policy claims.

Tips and Reminders:

1. Purchase travel insurance as soon as you book your trip to ensure coverage for trip cancellations or interruptions.

2. Read policy documents carefully and understand what's covered and what's not.

3. Disclose pre-existing medical conditions and provide accurate information when purchasing the policy.

4. Keep policy documents and contact information handy during your trip.

By investing in travel insurance, you'll be protected from unexpected expenses and able to enjoy your Brazilian adventure with peace of mind. Remember, travel insurance is not just a precaution, it's a necessity for a worry-free journey.

Good Travel Insurance Companies for Brazil

1. Allianz Travel Insurance

2. AXA Travel Insurance

3. TravelGuard Travel Insurance

4. Travelex Travel Insurance

5. Squaremouth Travel Insurance

These companies offer comprehensive travel insurance policies that meet Brazil's requirements and provide additional benefits such as emergency assistance, language support, and claim assistance.

Flights and Transportation

Several airlines operate flights to this vibrant destination, including:

- LATAM Airlines: Prices start from $800 USD (round-trip)
- American Airlines: Prices start from $850 USD (round-trip)
- Delta Air Lines: Prices start from $900 USD (round-trip)

Domestic Flights for Seamless Travel

Once arrived, domestic flights are an efficient way to explore the country. Consider the following airlines:

- Azul Airlines: Prices start from $100 USD (one-way)
- LATAM Airlines: Prices start from $120 USD (one-way)
- Gol Transportes Aéreos: Prices start from $80 USD (one-way)

Bus Transportation for Scenic Routes

The bus network is an affordable and efficient way to explore scenic routes. Companies like:

- Greyhound: Prices start from $20 USD (one-way)
- Ormeño: Prices start from $25 USD (one-way)

Convenient Taxi and Ride-hailing Services

Taxis and ride-hailing services are widely available. Consider:

- Uber: Prices start from $5 USD (one-way)
- 99Taxis: Prices start from $6 USD (one-way)

Rental Cars for Flexibility

Rental cars are a convenient way to explore. Companies like:

- Hertz: Prices start from $40 USD (per day)
- Avis: Prices start from $45 USD (per day)

Reputable Travel Companies

- Expedia: Offers a range of flights, hotels, and packages
- trivago: Specializes in accommodation bookings

Tips and Reminders

- Research transportation options before arriving

- Plan ahead and book tickets or rentals in advance

- Stay informed about local transportation strikes or disruptions

- Be mindful of your belongings and personal safety in crowded transportation hubs

Accommodation Options

Accommodation is a crucial aspect of any traveler's journey, and Brazil offers a diverse range of options to suit every style and budget. From budget-friendly hostels to luxurious resorts, travelers can find their perfect home away from home in this vibrant country.

Accommodation Options for Budget-Conscious Travelers

For travelers on a shoestring, hostels are an excellent choice. Not only are they affordable, but they also offer a great opportunity to meet fellow travelers and make new friends. Many hostels offer dormitory-style accommodation, as well as private rooms, and often have communal kitchens, lounges, and outdoor spaces. Some popular hostel options include:

1. Orixás Art Hostel in Salvador, with its colorful decor and lively atmosphere (R$ 60 - R$ 120 per night)
2. Rio Hostel in Rio de Janeiro, offering stunning views of Sugarloaf Mountain (R$ 80 - R$ 150 per night)

3. São Paulo Hostel, located in the heart of the city's vibrant Vila Madalena neighborhood (R$ 50 - R$ 100 per night)

Mid-Range Accommodation Options

For travelers seeking a little more comfort and privacy, mid-range hotels and pousadas (guesthouses) are an excellent choice. These charming establishments often offer cozy rooms, delicious breakfasts, and personalized service. Some standout options include:

1. Pousada do Rio in Rio de Janeiro, with its elegant rooms and beautiful gardens (R$ 250 - R$ 400 per night)
2. Hotel Casa do Amarelindo in Salvador, offering stunning views of the city (R$ 300 - R$ 500 per night)
3. Hotel Fasano in São Paulo, with its sleek design and top-notch amenities (R$ 400 - R$ 600 per night)

Luxury Accommodation Options

For travelers seeking the ultimate in comfort and luxury, high-end hotels and resorts are truly unforgettable. With lavish amenities, world-class service, and breathtaking views, these establishments will make you feel like royalty. Some top picks include:

1. Belmond Copacabana Palace in Rio de Janeiro, with its iconic art deco design and impeccable service (R$ 1,000 - R$ 2,000 per night)

2. Hotel Unique in São Paulo, offering sleek rooms and a rooftop pool with stunning views (R$ 800 - R$ 1,500 per night)

3. UXUA Casa Hotel in Trancoso, with its luxurious villas and private pools (R$ 1,200 - R$ 2,500 per night)

Alternative Accommodation Options

For travelers seeking something a little out of the ordinary, consider staying in a boutique hotel, eco-lodge, or even a houseboat! These unique options offer an immersive experience, allowing you to connect with the local culture and environment in a truly special way. Some highlights include:

1. Ariau Amazon Towers in Manaus, offering luxurious treehouse-style accommodation amidst the Amazon rainforest (R$ 500 - R$ 1,000 per night)
2. Casa do Lago in Fernando de Noronha, with its stunning lake views and eco-friendly design (R$ 400 - R$ 800 per night)
3. Houseboat Amazonas in Iquitos, allowing you to explore the Amazon River in style (R$ 300 - R$ 600 per night)

Tips and Tricks

When booking your accommodation, be sure to research thoroughly and read reviews from fellow travelers. Consider factors like location, safety, and amenities, and don't hesitate to reach out to the establishment directly with any questions or concerns. Also, be aware that prices may vary depending on the season and availability.

Chapter 2: Destinations

Rio de Janeiro

Rio de Janeiro, often referred to simply as "Rio," is a vibrant, iconic city that perfectly balances the energy of urban life with the tranquility of nature. Known for its golden beaches, pulsating samba beats, and dramatic landscapes, Rio continues to captivate travelers from around the globe. This dynamic metropolis offers an unforgettable mix of cultural, historical, and natural experiences, making it a must-visit destination for anyone heading to Brazil.

Getting to Rio de Janeiro

Rio de Janeiro is serviced by two main airports: Galeão International Airport (GIG) and Santos Dumont Airport (SDU). Most international flights arrive at Galeão, about 20 kilometers north of the city center. You can expect to pay around R$60-100 for a taxi or a ride-hailing service like Uber from Galeão to neighborhoods like Copacabana, Ipanema, or Leblon, where most tourists prefer to stay.

Public transportation is also available in the form of buses and the Metro, but for those unfamiliar with the city, a taxi or Uber is generally safer and more convenient. There are also shuttle services, with prices ranging from R$25 to R$50 depending on your final destination.

Best Time to Visit

The best time to visit Rio is between December and March, during the Brazilian summer when temperatures average between 25°C to 35°C (77°F to 95°F). This is also when the city hosts its famous Carnival celebration, which typically falls in February or early March. However, this is peak season, so expect higher prices and large crowds.

For those looking for milder weather and fewer tourists, visiting between April and October can offer a more relaxed experience. Prices for accommodations tend to drop by 20-30% during the off-season, making it an ideal time for budget travelers.

Iconic Landmarks

1. Christ the Redeemer (Cristo Redentor)

No visit to Rio would be complete without seeing Christ the Redeemer, one of the New Seven Wonders of the World. Perched atop Corcovado Mountain, this 30-meter-tall statue offers stunning panoramic views of the city. Tickets to visit Christ the Redeemer range from R$40 to R$90, depending on the season and whether you choose to take the train or a van up the mountain.

2. Sugarloaf Mountain (Pão de Açúcar)

Another must-visit landmark is Sugarloaf Mountain, which offers one of the most breathtaking views in all of Rio. You can take a cable car to the top, with tickets costing around R$120 for adults. The two-stage ride provides sweeping views of the Atlantic Ocean, Guanabara Bay, and Rio's downtown. For adventure seekers, there are also hiking and rock-climbing opportunities available.

3. Copacabana and Ipanema Beaches

Rio's beaches are as famous as its landmarks. Copacabana and Ipanema are the most well-known and are excellent spots to experience the city's vibrant beach culture. Whether you're sunbathing, playing beach volleyball, or simply enjoying a fresh coconut (which costs around R$6-8), these beaches are free to access and ideal for both relaxation and people-watching.

If you're visiting on a Sunday, don't miss the open-air markets along Ipanema's Hippie Fair (Feira Hippie de Ipanema), where you can buy locally made arts, crafts, and souvenirs. Prices for goods can vary, but expect to spend anywhere from R$30 to R$200 depending on the item.

4. Lapa Arches (Arcos da Lapa) and the Selarón Steps (Escadaria Selarón)

For a taste of Rio's bohemian spirit, head to Lapa, a neighborhood known for its lively nightlife and cultural scene. Here, you'll find the iconic Lapa Arches, a historical aqueduct, and the colorful Selarón Steps, a mosaic staircase created by Chilean-born artist Jorge Selarón. Both sites are free to visit, though a guided walking tour, which can range from R$50 to R$100, can provide a deeper understanding of the area's history and culture.

Cultural Experiences

1. Carnival

Rio de Janeiro's Carnival is world-renowned, attracting millions of tourists each year. Even if you're not in Rio during the official Carnival period, you can still experience samba and Carnival culture year-round at Sambadrome parades or by visiting samba schools. The cost for a night at a samba school or a Carnival-themed party ranges from R$100 to R$500, depending on the venue and event.

2. Museum of Tomorrow (Museu do Amanhã)

One of Rio's newest and most innovative attractions is the Museum of Tomorrow, located in the revitalized Porto Maravilha area. The museum, housed in a futuristic building designed by Spanish architect Santiago Calatrava, focuses on sustainability and technological innovation. Admission costs around R$30, and the museum is a great way to spend a few hours learning about global challenges in an interactive environment.

3. Maracanã Stadium

For football enthusiasts, a visit to Maracanã Stadium is a must. This iconic stadium has hosted numerous historic football matches, including the 2014 World Cup final. Guided tours cost around R$50, and you can even attend a local football match if you're lucky, with tickets ranging from R$60 to R$150 depending on the game.

Dining in Rio de Janeiro

Brazilian cuisine is rich, varied, and Rio is no exception. The city offers everything from high-end dining experiences to street food. A popular traditional dish is feijoada, a black bean stew served with rice, collard greens, and pork. You can find feijoada at most traditional restaurants for around R$40 to R$70 per person.

If you're in the mood for a casual snack, try a coxinha, a fried dough ball filled with shredded chicken. These are typically sold at bakeries or street vendors for R$5 to R$8 each.

For a splurge-worthy dining experience, head to one of Rio's churrascarias (Brazilian steakhouses), where waiters serve endless cuts of grilled meats directly at your table. A meal at a mid-range churrascaria will cost around R$120 to R$200 per person.

Safety Tips

While Rio is an incredible destination, it's important to stay mindful of your surroundings. Petty crime, particularly pickpocketing, can be an issue in crowded areas and on public transportation. Stick to well-lit, populated areas, especially at night, and avoid wearing expensive jewelry or flashing large amounts of cash.

Consider using a money belt or a secure bag when walking around the city. For safer travel, use Uber instead of taxis, and stay in neighborhoods like Copacabana, Ipanema, or

Leblon, which are well-policed and have plenty of amenities for tourists.

São Paulo

São Paulo, Brazil's largest city, is a dynamic urban center brimming with culture, cuisine, and a diverse array of experiences. As the economic heart of Brazil, São Paulo offers travelers a compelling blend of history, modernity, and cosmopolitan flair. This guide provides an in-depth look at what to expect when visiting São Paulo, including key attractions, culinary delights, and practical tips, all with current pricing information in Brazilian Real (R$).

Key Attractions

1. Avenida Paulista

Avenida Paulista is the city's cultural and financial artery. This bustling avenue is lined with historic buildings, museums, and cultural institutions. The São Paulo Museum of Art (MASP), located at number 1578, is a highlight with its impressive collection of Western art. Admission costs around R$50. The nearby Japan House, a cultural center dedicated to Japanese art and technology, offers free entry.

2. Ibirapuera Park

One of São Paulo's largest green spaces, Ibirapuera Park is a sanctuary of nature amidst the urban sprawl. Covering over 1,500 acres, the park features walking trails, lakes, and several museums, including the Museum of Modern Art (MAM) and the Afro-Brazil Museum. Entrance to the park is free, though museum entry varies, with MAM charging about R$25.

3. Mercado Municipal

The Mercado Municipal, or Mercadão, is an essential stop for food lovers. Famous for its mortadella sandwich and exotic fruits, this market offers a sensory overload of sights and smells. Expect to pay around R$30 for a sandwich and varying prices for fresh produce and gourmet items.

4. Liberdade

São Paulo's Japanese neighborhood, Liberdade, is a cultural enclave showcasing Japanese traditions and cuisine. Wander through its bustling streets, visit the Japanese immigration museum (admission around R$20), and savor authentic sushi or ramen in one of the many restaurants.

5. São Paulo Cathedral

Located in Praça da Sé, the São Paulo Cathedral is a stunning example of neo-Gothic architecture. The cathedral, a landmark in the city's historic center, offers free entry and provides a peaceful retreat from the hustle of the city.

Culinary Scene

1. D.O.M.

For an unforgettable fine dining experience, D.O.M. by Chef Alex Atala is a must-visit. This restaurant, frequently listed among the world's top, offers a menu that celebrates Brazilian ingredients with a modern twist. Expect to spend around R$600 per person for a tasting menu.

2. Figueira Rubaiyat

Known for its impressive fig tree in the center of the restaurant, Figueira Rubaiyat offers an exceptional dining experience with a focus on quality meats and Brazilian cuisine. A meal here can cost between R$250 and R$400 per person.

3. Cantina do Piero

For a more casual yet authentic Italian meal, Cantina do Piero provides hearty pasta dishes and traditional fare. Prices are more accessible, with main courses costing between R$50 and R$100.

4. Vila Madalena

This bohemian neighborhood is known for its vibrant nightlife and eclectic dining options. Explore the array of bars, cafes, and street food vendors offering everything from gourmet burgers to traditional Brazilian snacks.

Shopping

1. Rua Oscar Freire

This upscale shopping street is São Paulo's answer to Rodeo Drive, featuring luxury boutiques and high-end brands. Prices for designer items vary widely, but it's the perfect place to indulge in luxury shopping.

2. 25 de Março Street

For a more budget-friendly shopping experience, 25 de Março Street is the place to go. This bustling market area offers everything from fashion to electronics at competitive prices. Be prepared for a lively, crowded environment.

Practical Information

1. Transportation

São Paulo's public transportation system includes buses, metro, and trains. A single metro or bus ticket costs around R$5. Taxis and ride-sharing services are also readily available, with rates starting around R$10 for base fare and increasing with distance.

2. Accommodation

São Paulo offers a wide range of accommodation options:

Luxury: The Hotel Unique, known for its distinctive architecture and excellent service, charges around R$800 per night.

Mid-Range: The Pullman São Paulo Vila Olímpia offers comfort and convenience at approximately R$300 per night.

Budget: For a more economical stay, consider hostels like the Samba Rooms Hostel, with rates starting around R$ 80 per night for a dormitory bed.

3. Safety and Health

São Paulo is generally safe for tourists, but like any large city, it's wise to stay alert and be cautious with personal belongings. It is recommended to use sunscreen and stay hydrated, especially during the hot summer months (December to March). Tap water is generally safe to drink, but bottled water is widely available.

Amazon Rainforest

The Amazon Rainforest, a sprawling expanse of verdant wilderness, is a destination of unparalleled intrigue and ecological significance. Spanning across nine countries in South America, this colossal forest covers over 5.5 million square kilometers, with the majority of it residing in Brazil. For travelers visiting Brazil, the Amazon offers a unique opportunity to immerse themselves in one of the world's most biodiverse ecosystems.

The Amazon Rainforest is often described as the "lungs of the Earth" due to its vast capacity to produce oxygen and absorb carbon dioxide. Its rich tapestry of flora and fauna creates an ecosystem unlike any other, making it a prime destination for eco-tourists and nature enthusiasts. The forest is home to an estimated 390 billion individual trees, representing around 16,000 species. This incredible biodiversity supports a multitude of wildlife, including jaguars, sloths, and over 1,300 bird species.

Key Attractions and Activities

1. Wildlife Viewing: The Amazon is renowned for its diverse wildlife. Guided tours offer the chance to spot elusive creatures such as the Amazon river dolphin, capuchin monkeys, and vibrant parrots. Early morning and late afternoon are prime times for wildlife sightings, as many animals are more active during these cooler periods.

2. River Cruises: One of the most popular ways to explore the Amazon is via river cruises. These cruises allow travelers to navigate the waterways of the rainforest, offering views of lush landscapes and opportunities to visit remote indigenous communities. Luxury cruises offer spacious cabins and gourmet meals, while more basic options provide a closer connection to nature.

3. Canopy Walkways: For a different perspective of the rainforest, canopy walkways provide a bird's-eye view of the forest floor. Suspended high above the ground, these walkways offer breathtaking vistas and a unique vantage point to observe the canopy layer where many species of birds and insects reside.

4. Jungle Treks: For the adventurous, guided jungle treks offer an immersive experience. These treks can vary in length and difficulty, from short walks to multi-day expeditions. Guides provide valuable insights into the local flora and fauna, and trekkers may have the chance to learn survival skills and traditional uses of plants.

5. Cultural Encounters: Visiting indigenous communities provides a rich cultural experience. Many communities welcome visitors and offer insights into their traditional ways of life, including craftsmanship, dance, and culinary practices. These interactions foster a deeper understanding of the symbiotic relationship between the people and their environment.

Practical Information

1. Best Time to Visit: The Amazon Rainforest can be visited year-round, but the climate varies significantly between the wet and dry seasons. The dry season (May to October) is generally considered the best time for travel due to lower humidity and reduced rainfall, making outdoor activities more enjoyable.

The wet season (November to April) brings heavier rains and higher humidity, but also increases river levels, which can enhance river cruise experiences.

2. Tours and Guides: Numerous tour operators offer guided experiences in the Amazon. Day tours generally cost between R$ 300 and R$ 700 per person, while multi-day packages can range from R$ 2,000 to R$ 6,000, depending on the level of comfort and inclusivity. It is advisable to book tours in advance, especially during peak travel seasons.

3. Health and Safety: Travelers should be aware of potential health risks, including mosquito-borne diseases such as malaria and dengue fever. Vaccinations for hepatitis A, B, and typhoid are recommended, and malaria prophylaxis may be necessary. It is also important to use insect repellent and wear protective clothing.

4. Travel Essentials: Pack light, breathable clothing, sturdy hiking boots, and rain gear. Binoculars and a good camera are essential for wildlife viewing. Due to

the high humidity, travelers should also bring waterproof bags to protect their belongings.

Northeast Brazil (Salvador, Fernando de Noronha)

Northeast Brazil is a region of striking contrasts and vivid experiences, encompassing vibrant urban centers and tranquil natural paradises. Among its most captivating destinations are Salvador, the historic and cultural heart of Bahia, and Fernando de Noronha, an idyllic archipelago renowned for its pristine natural beauty.

Salvador: A Cultural and Historical Jewel

Salvador, the capital of Bahia, is a city where history, culture, and art converge. Founded in 1549, it was Brazil's first colonial capital and remains a vibrant showcase of African-influenced Brazilian culture. Salvador's charm lies in its colorful streets, historical landmarks, and dynamic cultural scene.

Pelourinho: The Historic Heart of Salvador

Pelourinho, often referred to as "Pelô," is Salvador's historic district and a UNESCO World Heritage site. The area is famous for its colonial architecture, including ornate churches and brightly painted buildings. The São Francisco Church, with its lavish baroque interior and intricate woodwork, is a must-see. Adjacent to the church, the Igreja do Carmo offers a more subdued yet equally captivating experience with its serene atmosphere and historical artifacts.

Pelourinho is also home to several museums that provide insight into Salvador's rich heritage. The Museum of Brazilian Art (Museu de Arte da Bahia) showcases a collection of Brazilian art from the colonial period to the present day. Similarly, the Museum of Religion (Museu de Religiosidade) offers a fascinating look into the spiritual and cultural practices that shape the city's diverse religious landscape.

Price Range:

- Pelourinho Guided Tours: R$120 - R$220 per person
- Museum Entrance Fees: R$20 - R$40 per person
- Elevador Lacerda and Mercado Modelo

The Elevador Lacerda is an iconic Salvador landmark, connecting the lower city to the upper city with its impressive vertical lift. The elevator provides panoramic views of the Bay of All Saints, making it an excellent vantage point for photography.

At the base of the Elevador Lacerda lies Mercado Modelo, a bustling market where visitors can shop for local crafts, souvenirs, and sample traditional Bahian cuisine. The market's vibrant atmosphere is a sensory feast, with stalls offering everything from handcrafted jewelry to spicy street food.

Price Range:

- Elevador Lacerda Ride: Included with the entry fee of around R$15 - R$30 for various attractions
- Market Shopping: Variable, with souvenirs ranging from R$20 - R$200

Beaches and Coastal Attractions

Salvador's coastline is adorned with stunning beaches that cater to various interests. Porto da Barra Beach, located in the heart of the city, is known for its calm waters and historical significance as one of Salvador's first public beaches. It's an ideal spot for swimming and relaxation.

For a more secluded experience, the beaches of Flamengo and Stella Maris, situated to the south of the city, offer pristine sands and clear waters. These beaches are perfect for a day trip, providing opportunities for sunbathing, swimming, and enjoying local seafood.

Price Range:

- Porto da Barra Beach: Free
- Day Trip to Flamengo or Stella Maris: R$50 - R$100 for transportation

Fernando de Noronha: A Natural Paradise

Fernando de Noronha, an archipelago off Brazil's northeastern coast, is renowned for its exceptional natural beauty and marine biodiversity. It offers a unique blend of pristine beaches, crystal-clear waters, and rich wildlife, making it a premier destination for eco-tourism and adventure.

Praia do Sancho: The Crown Jewel

Praia do Sancho is often cited as one of the world's most beautiful beaches. Accessible via a staircase carved into the cliffs, it features golden sands and turquoise waters. The beach is perfect for swimming, snorkeling, and simply soaking in the breathtaking scenery. Its secluded nature ensures a tranquil experience, with limited visitor numbers regulated to preserve its pristine condition.

Price Range:

- Entrance Fee to Fernando de Noronha National Marine Park: R$150 - R$250 per person (includes access to Praia do Sancho)

Diving and Snorkeling Adventures

Fernando de Noronha is a top destination for diving and snorkeling, thanks to its clear waters and diverse marine life. The island's waters are home to various species, including sea turtles, dolphins, and colorful fish. Diving tours often include visits to coral reefs and underwater caves, while snorkeling offers the chance to observe marine life in shallower waters.

Popular diving spots include the shipwreck of the Corveta V 17 and the rich coral formations around Atalaia Beach. These experiences are guided by local experts who ensure both safety and an immersive exploration of the underwater world.

Price Range:

- Diving Tour: R$600 - R$1,200 per person
- Snorkeling Tour: R$200 - R$400 per person

Eco-Tours and Hiking

For those interested in land-based activities, Fernando de Noronha offers numerous eco-tours and hiking opportunities. Trails like the one to the Mirante dos Golfinhos provide stunning views of the coastline and opportunities to spot dolphins and other marine wildlife.

The island's commitment to conservation means that eco-tours are designed to minimize impact while enhancing the visitor experience. These tours often include educational components about the island's unique ecosystem and conservation efforts.

Price Range:

- Eco-Tours and Hiking: R$150 - R$300 per person

South Brazil (Florianópolis, Iguaçu Falls)

South Brazil is a region known for its stunning natural landscapes and vibrant cultural scene, making it a compelling destination for travelers seeking both adventure and relaxation. Two standout locations in this region are Florianópolis and Iguaçu Falls. Each offers a unique experience, from pristine beaches and bustling markets to breathtaking waterfalls and lush rainforests.

Florianópolis: The Enchanting Island City

Florianópolis, often affectionately called "Floripa," is a dynamic city located on Santa Catarina Island. Renowned for its beautiful beaches, rich cultural heritage, and lively atmosphere, Florianópolis is a must-visit destination.

Beaches and Outdoor Activities

Florianópolis boasts some of the best beaches in Brazil. Praia Mole and Joaquina Beach are particularly popular among surfers due to their strong waves and vibrant surf culture. Praia Mole, with its golden sands and clear waters, is perfect for sunbathing and swimming. For a quieter experience, Lagoa da Conceição offers serene views and opportunities for kayaking and paddleboarding. The cost of beach access is free, though some activities like surf rentals can range from R$ 60 to R$ 150 per day.

Cultural and Historical Sites

The city's historical charm is evident in its architecture and cultural sites. The Centro Histórico features colonial-era buildings, such as the Cathedral of Florianópolis and the 19th-century Public Market. The market is a vibrant hub where visitors can sample local delicacies like "pastéis" (fried pastries) and fresh seafood. A meal at the market typically costs between R$ 40 and R$ 80. Additionally, the "Forte Sant'Anna" and the "Catedral Metropolitana" offer insights into the city's past. Entry to these historical sites is generally free or has a nominal fee of around R$ 10 to R$ 20.

Local Cuisine and Dining

Florianópolis is known for its seafood, and dining here is an experience not to be missed. The city's restaurants and beachside kiosks offer a range of dishes, from the famous "sequência de camarão" (shrimp sequence) to "moqueca" (a Brazilian seafood stew). Prices for meals at mid-range restaurants can vary from R$ 80 to R$ 150 per person.

Iguaçu Falls: A Natural Wonder

Located on the border between Brazil and Argentina, Iguaçu Falls is one of the most awe-inspiring natural attractions in the world. This massive waterfall system comprises approximately 275 individual falls, creating a spectacular display of nature's power and beauty.

The Falls and National Parks

The Iguaçu Falls are divided between the Brazilian side and the Argentine side, with the Brazilian side offering panoramic views and the Argentine side providing close-up experiences. The Brazilian side's visitor center includes a network of walkways and viewing platforms that offer breathtaking vistas of the falls. A ticket to the Iguaçu National Park on the Brazilian side costs around R$ 80 to R$ 120. The Argentine side, accessible via the Parque Nacional Iguazú, also charges an entrance fee, generally ranging from ARS 2,500 to ARS 3,500 (about R$ 80 to R$ 120).

Boat Tours and Activities

For an adrenaline-filled experience, consider taking a boat tour that gets you close to the base of the falls. These tours are available from both the Brazilian and Argentine sides and cost between R$ 250 and R$ 400. The boat ride, known locally as "Macuco Safari," is an exhilarating way to experience the power of the falls and often includes a waterfall drenching that enhances the thrill.

Wildlife and Nature Trails

The surrounding Iguaçu National Park is also a haven for wildlife enthusiasts. The park is home to a diverse range of animals, including toucans, capuchin monkeys, and coatis. Guided nature trails offer insights into the local flora and fauna. Tours that include wildlife spotting and trekking can range from R$ 150 to R$ 300, depending on the length and type of the tour.

Cultural Experiences

In addition to natural attractions, the area around Iguaçu Falls offers cultural experiences such as visiting local communities and learning about the indigenous Guarani culture. These cultural tours typically cost between R$ 150 and R$ 250 and provide a deeper understanding of the region's heritage.

Practical Travel Tips

1. Traveling to Florianópolis

Florianópolis is accessible via its international airport, Hercílio Luz Airport (FLN), which is well-connected to major cities in Brazil. Domestic flights from São Paulo or Rio de Janeiro are frequent and typically cost between R$ 400 and R$ 700 for a round-trip ticket.

2. Traveling to Iguaçu Falls

The Iguaçu Falls can be reached via Foz do Iguaçu International Airport (IGU). This airport has connections to various Brazilian cities, and flights usually range from R$ 500 to R$ 800 for a round-trip ticket. From the airport, visitors can take taxis or shuttle services to the falls.

3. Best Time to Visit

The best time to visit Florianópolis is between December and March when the weather is warm and ideal for beach activities. Iguaçu Falls is best visited during the rainy season (November to March) when the water flow is at its highest, though this can also mean more tourists.

In summary, South Brazil, with its blend of natural wonders and cultural richness, offers an unforgettable experience. Whether exploring the beaches of Florianópolis or marveling at the grandeur of Iguaçu Falls, travelers are guaranteed to find adventure, relaxation, and a deep appreciation for this remarkable part of the world.

Brasília and the Federal District

Brasília, the capital of Brazil, is a city like no other. Built from scratch in the 1950s, this modernist metropolis is a UNESCO World Heritage Site and a must-visit destination for travelers. Located in the Federal District, Brasília is a hub of culture, history, and innovation, offering a unique blend of attractions and experiences.

Must-visit attractions:

1. Cathedral of Brasília: R$ 10 (USD 2.50) per person
- A stunning example of modernist architecture, with breathtaking views of the city.
2. National Museum of the Republic: R$ 15 (USD 3.75) per person
- Showcasing Brazil's history, art, and culture, with interactive exhibits and artifacts.
3. Three Powers Square: Free admission
- The heart of Brasília's government district, featuring iconic buildings and monuments.

Other Federal District Destinations

1. Planaltina: A charming town with historic architecture and natural springs
2. Ceilândia: A vibrant neighborhood with street art, markets, and local cuisine
3. Paranoá Lake: A scenic spot for boating, fishing, and relaxation

Activities and Experiences

1. Guided city tours: R$ 50-100 (USD 12.50-25) per person
2. Visit to the TV Tower: R$ 20-30 (USD 5-7.50) per person
3. Exploration of the Federal District's natural parks: Free admission

Cuisine

Brasília's cuisine is a fusion of traditional Brazilian flavors with modern twists. Be sure to try:

1. Feijoada: R$ 30-50 (USD 7.50-12.50) per serving

2. Churrasco: R$ 40-60 (USD 10-15) per serving

3. Pão de Queijo: R$ 10-15 (USD 2.50-3.75) per serving

Tips and Reminders

1. Research and plan ahead to avoid peak season prices

2. Respect local customs and traditions

3. Be mindful of personal safety and belongings in crowded areas

Chapter 3: Experiences

Beaches and Coastlines

Brazil's coastlines and beaches are among the most celebrated in the world, offering an array of experiences from tranquil getaways to vibrant party scenes. Stretching over 7,000 kilometers, Brazil's coastal region presents a diverse array of landscapes and activities that cater to every type of traveler. Whether you seek serene shores, thrilling water sports, or cultural immersion, Brazil's beaches promise an unforgettable experience.

1. Copacabana Beach, Rio de Janeiro

Copacabana Beach, situated in the heart of Rio de Janeiro, is one of the most iconic beaches in Brazil. Known for its golden sands and lively atmosphere, this beach is a hub of activity both day and night. Visitors can enjoy sunbathing, beach volleyball, or a stroll along the 4 km-long promenade, designed with distinctive black-and-white wave patterns.

Activities and Costs:

- Beach Volleyball: R$ 40 - R$ 80 per hour (rental of equipment and space)
- Beach Chairs and Umbrellas: R$ 20 - R$ 50 per day
- Local Street Food: R$ 10 - R$ 30 per item

The area around Copacabana offers a range of dining and shopping options, making it ideal for those who want a mix of beach time and urban exploration.

2. Ipanema Beach, Rio de Janeiro

Ipanema Beach, a short distance from Copacabana, is famed for its sophisticated ambiance and clear waters. This beach is divided into different "postos" or lifeguard stations, each catering to specific crowds, such as families, sports enthusiasts, or the LGBTQ+ community. Ipanema's vibrant beach scene is complemented by a rich array of bars and restaurants.

Activities and Costs:

- Surf Lessons: R$ 100 - R$ 200 per session

- Stand-Up Paddleboarding: R$ 80 - R$ 150 per hour
- Beachfront Cafés: R$ 30 - R$ 100 per meal

Ipanema's proximity to upscale shopping and dining makes it a hotspot for those wanting a blend of luxury and beach relaxation.

3. Praia do Forte, Bahia

Praia do Forte, located in the state of Bahia, is renowned for its picturesque beauty and ecological significance. The beach is part of a protected area where visitors can observe sea turtles at the Tamar Project, a conservation initiative aimed at protecting endangered species.

Activities and Costs:

- Turtle Watching Tours: R$ 60 - R$ 120 per person
- Snorkeling: R$ 70 - R$ 150 per tour
- Local Seafood Restaurants: R$ 50 - R$ 150 per meal

The serene environment of Praia do Forte makes it ideal for nature enthusiasts and those looking to escape the bustling city life.

4. Jericoacoara, Ceará

Jericoacoara, often referred to as "Jeri," is a remote beach town located in the state of Ceará. Known for its stunning natural beauty, Jericoacoara offers dramatic sand dunes, crystal-clear lagoons, and a laid-back vibe. It is a popular destination for windsurfing and kitesurfing due to its favorable wind conditions.

Activities and Costs:

- Kitesurfing Lessons: R$ 200 - R$ 400 per session
- Dune Buggy Rides: R$ 150 - R$ 300 per hour
- Sunset Tours: R$ 80 - R$ 150 per person

Jeri's relaxed atmosphere and stunning landscapes make it a paradise for adventure seekers and those wanting a more tranquil beach experience.

5. Florianópolis, Santa Catarina

Florianópolis, often called "Magic Island," is famous for its diverse beaches, ranging from lively urban stretches to secluded coves. With over 40 beaches, this island city offers something for every beachgoer. Popular spots include Praia Mole and Joaquina Beach, both known for their excellent surfing conditions.

Activities and Costs:

- Surfing Lessons: R$ 120 - R$ 250 per session
- Beachfront Bars: R$ 30 - R$ 70 per drink
- Boat Tours: R$ 100 - R$ 200 per tour

Florianópolis combines vibrant beach life with opportunities for outdoor activities, making it a great destination for those who enjoy a mix of relaxation and adventure.

6. Porto de Galinhas, Pernambuco

Porto de Galinhas, located in Pernambuco, is renowned for its natural pools formed by coral reefs. These pools create a unique snorkeling experience, where visitors can swim among colorful fish and marine life. The town itself is charming, with cobblestone streets and local crafts.

Activities and Costs:

- Snorkeling in Natural Pools: R$ 50 - R$ 100 per tour

- Beachfront Crafts Market: R$ 20 - R$ 100 per item
- Local Cuisine: R$ 40 - R$ 120 per meal

Porto de Galinhas is perfect for those interested in marine life and enjoying a quaint, picturesque beach town.

7. Baia do Sancho, Fernando de Noronha

Baia do Sancho, on the Fernando de Noronha archipelago, is often cited as one of the world's most beautiful beaches. Its turquoise waters, dramatic cliffs, and rich marine life make it a top destination for divers and nature lovers. Accessing the beach involves a steep descent, but the stunning views and clear waters are worth the effort.

Activities and Costs:

- Scuba Diving: R$ 300 - R$ 600 per dive
- Boat Tours to Nearby Beaches: R$ 150 - R$ 300 per tour
- Entrance Fee to the Island: R$ 75 - R$ 150 per day

Fernando de Noronha's exclusivity and natural beauty make it a premium destination for those seeking an extraordinary beach experience.

Outdoor Adventures (Hiking, Surfing)

For travelers seeking an adrenaline-packed experience, hiking and surfing are two of the most thrilling outdoor adventures to embark on. With its vast wilderness areas, rugged coastlines, and consistent waves, the perfect setting for these activities awaits.

Hiking Through the Amazon Rainforest

The Amazon Rainforest, often referred to as the "lungs of the Earth," is an awe-inspiring destination for hiking aficionados. Embarking on a guided hike through this dense, tropical rainforest offers an immersive experience into one of the world's most biodiverse ecosystems.

Typical guided hikes in the Amazon range from half-day excursions to multi-day treks. A half-day tour, which usually includes a guide, basic equipment, and refreshments, costs around R$200 to R$400 per person. For those seeking a more extensive adventure, multi-day treks that include camping in the forest and meals can cost between R$1,500 and R$4,000, depending on the level of luxury and the length of the expedition.

As you traverse winding trails and encounter towering trees, you'll be accompanied by guides who share their knowledge about the flora, fauna, and indigenous cultures. Keep an eye out for exotic wildlife such as jaguars, capuchin monkeys, and vibrant toucans, and listen to the cacophony of the forest's natural soundtrack. These hikes not only offer physical challenges but also provide a profound appreciation for the delicate balance of this crucial environment.

Trekking the Pantanal Wetlands

Another remarkable hiking destination is the Pantanal, the world's largest tropical wetland. Unlike the dense canopy of the Amazon, the Pantanal features open landscapes with expansive floodplains, grasslands, and seasonal wetlands. This environment offers a different set of hiking experiences, such as bird watching and wildlife spotting.

Day hikes in the Pantanal can cost approximately R$300 to R$600 per person. Multi-day safaris that include guided hikes, boat rides, and accommodation in lodges or camping sites range from R$2,000 to R$5,000. This region is renowned for its incredible biodiversity, including the elusive jaguar, capybaras, and a plethora of bird species. Hikers here are treated to a panoramic view of this unique ecosystem and can experience the seasonal changes of the wetlands.

Surfing Along Brazil's Atlantic Coast

Brazil's coastline stretches over 7,000 kilometers, offering an array of surfing opportunities for all skill levels. The country's surf culture is vibrant, with some of the world's most renowned breaks found in both the northeast and southeast regions.

Northeast Brazil is famous for its consistent and powerful waves. Cities like Fortaleza and Natal provide excellent conditions for surfers. A typical surf lesson or equipment rental in these areas costs between R$150 and R$300 for a session, which usually includes a board, wetsuit, and instruction. More advanced surfers can explore iconic breaks like Canoa Quebrada, where daily rates for surf rentals are around R$100 to R$200.

Southeast Brazil, including destinations such as Rio de Janeiro and São Paulo, also boasts superb surf spots. The beaches of Rio, such as Ipanema and Copacabana, cater to surfers with varying skill levels. Surfing lessons here are priced similarly, ranging from R$150 to R$300, while equipment rental is around R$100 to R$150 per day. These locations offer not only great waves but also the vibrant urban backdrop of Brazil's cultural capital.

The South offers a different experience with spots like Floripa (Florianópolis), where the waves are more suited for intermediate to advanced surfers. Surf schools and equipment rentals here range from R$150 to R$300, and local surf shops offer boards for around R$100 to R$200 per day.

Enhancing Your Experience

For both hiking and surfing, travelers can enhance their experiences with local guides and instructors. In the Amazon and Pantanal, guides provide invaluable insights into the environment, making the journey not only enjoyable but educational. In surfing hotspots, instructors help improve technique and ensure safety, making the experience accessible to beginners and challenging for advanced surfers.

Travelers should also consider seasonal variations when planning their adventures. The Amazon is best explored during the dry season (June to November) when trails are more accessible, while the Pantanal's dry season (May to September) offers the best wildlife viewing. For surfing, the northeast coast has consistent waves year-round, while the southeast and south have seasonal swells that vary throughout the year.

Whether navigating the trails of the Amazon, spotting wildlife in the Pantanal, or riding the waves along Brazil's extensive coastline, outdoor adventures in this vibrant country offer something for every enthusiast. Each experience immerses travelers in Brazil's breathtaking natural beauty and dynamic culture, making it a destination that truly satisfies the spirit of adventure.

Cultural Experiences (Music, Dance)

For travelers seeking a rich tapestry of cultural experiences, Brazil offers a vibrant array of musical and dance traditions that reflect its diverse heritage. This country, known for its lively rhythms and colorful celebrations, provides an immersive experience for those eager to connect with its cultural heartbeat. Whether you're exploring the beats of samba or the intricate steps of capoeira, Brazil's cultural offerings are as varied as they are captivating.

Samba: The Soul of Brazil

Samba, arguably the most iconic of Brazilian musical styles, is deeply embedded in the nation's cultural fabric. Originating in Rio de Janeiro, samba is celebrated year-round, but its most famous manifestation is during Carnival. This festival, held annually in February or March, transforms Rio into a vibrant explosion of color and sound. The Sambadrome, a purpose-built parade venue, becomes the stage for elaborate parades featuring samba schools from across the city. Tickets for the Sambadrome vary in price, ranging from

R$100 to R$500 depending on the seating and the night of the event.

Beyond Carnival, samba can be experienced in numerous local venues. Samba clubs and bars, particularly in Rio's Lapa neighborhood, offer live performances that capture the essence of this rhythmic genre. Entrance fees typically range from R$50 to R$150, including a drink. For a more intimate experience, you might consider booking a samba class. These classes are widely available and cost between R$100 and R$200 for a session, providing a chance to learn the basics from seasoned instructors.

Bossa Nova: A Melodic Evolution

Bossa Nova, born in the late 1950s, represents a sophisticated evolution of samba. This genre, characterized by its smooth, melodic lines and gentle rhythms, was pioneered by artists like João Gilberto and Antônio Carlos Jobim. In Rio de Janeiro, you can experience live bossa nova performances at venues such as the Bossa Nova Lounge or the famous Vinícius Bar. Ticket prices for these performances generally range from R$80 to R$200, offering an elegant evening out for music enthusiasts.

Additionally, bossa nova remains a staple in many high-end restaurants and jazz clubs, where you can enjoy a meal accompanied by live music. These establishments often feature performances that blend bossa nova with other jazz influences, creating a sophisticated atmosphere. Expect to spend around R$200 to R$300 for an evening that includes dinner and entertainment.

Forró: The Dance of the Northeast

Traveling to Brazil's Northeast region opens up an opportunity to experience forró, a dance and musical genre rooted in the region's traditions. Forró, which incorporates elements of folk music and dance, is celebrated in festive gatherings and dance halls. In cities like Recife and Fortaleza, you'll find vibrant forró clubs and street festivals where locals and visitors come together to dance the night away.

Entrance to forró clubs typically costs between R$30 and R$100. If you're interested in learning forró, dance schools in these cities offer classes that usually cost around R$80 to R$150 per session. These classes are a fantastic way to immerse yourself in the regional culture and learn the steps that make forró so beloved.

Capoeira: The Dance-Fight Tradition

Capoeira, a unique blend of martial arts, dance, and music, is another distinctive aspect of Brazilian culture. Originally developed by African slaves, capoeira combines fluid dance movements with combat techniques and is accompanied by traditional instruments such as the berimbau (a single-string percussion instrument). Capoeira performances and rodas (circle dances) can be observed in various parts of Brazil, particularly in Salvador, where the tradition is deeply rooted.

Participating in a capoeira class is an excellent way to engage with this dynamic tradition. Classes are available in many cities and usually cost between R$100 and R$200. Observing a capoeira roda, which is often held in public squares or parks, is generally free, though some organized performances might charge an entrance fee ranging from R$50 to R$150.

Maracatu: A Rhythmic Extravaganza

Maracatu, an Afro-Brazilian tradition from Pernambuco, combines elaborate costumes, powerful rhythms, and dramatic performances. This tradition is most prominent during Carnival but can also be witnessed during various cultural festivals throughout the year. Maracatu parades feature large groups of performers drumming and dancing in vibrant, ceremonial attire.

Experiencing maracatu involves attending local festivals or parades, which are often free to the public. However, if you wish to participate in a maracatu workshop or tour, prices typically range from R$150 to R$300. These workshops provide an in-depth look at the music, dance, and cultural significance of maracatu.

Exploring Local Music Scenes

Aside from organized performances and festivals, Brazil's local music scenes offer intimate and authentic experiences. Small bars, cafes, and cultural centers across cities like São Paulo, Rio de Janeiro, and Salvador host live music nights featuring a range of genres from MPB (Música Popular Brasileira) to regional folk music. These venues provide a chance to experience Brazil's diverse musical landscape up close, with entrance fees generally ranging from R$30 to R$100.

In conclusion, Brazil's cultural landscape is a mosaic of musical and dance traditions that offer travelers an engaging and enriching experience. From the infectious rhythms of samba and the smooth tones of bossa nova to the energetic steps of forró and the dynamic performances of capoeira and maracatu, Brazil provides a wealth of opportunities for cultural exploration. Whether you're watching a grand Carnival parade or participating in a local dance class, the country's vibrant cultural offerings are sure to leave a lasting impression.

Food and Drink (Restaurants, Street Food)

Embarking on a culinary adventure in South America's largest country unveils an array of flavors that mirror its diverse culture and stunning landscapes. Travelers to this vibrant destination will find that food and drink are integral to the local experience, offering a blend of traditional dishes and modern twists that reflect the nation's rich heritage.

In the bustling metropolis of São Paulo, the street food scene provides an excellent starting point for any culinary journey. The city is renowned for its array of snacks and quick bites, each offering a unique taste of local life. A popular choice is the "pastel," a golden, deep-fried pastry with a flaky crust, often filled with a variety of ingredients such as cheese, minced meat, or even sweet fillings. These treats are widely available from street vendors and can cost between R$7 and R$15, making them both a delicious and affordable indulgence.

Another iconic street food is the "coxinha," a savory delight shaped like a teardrop and typically stuffed with seasoned chicken. These are often served with a side of spicy sauce and cost about R$6 to R$12 each. Accompanying these snacks with a refreshing glass of "caldo de cana" (sugarcane juice) enhances the experience. This sweet beverage is sold for around R$5 to R$10 and provides a cooling, natural sweetness that perfectly complements the savory flavors of the street food.

Venturing to Rio de Janeiro introduces travelers to a different culinary landscape, focused on fresh, coastal fare. One of the highlights is "feijoada," a traditional black bean stew cooked with various cuts of pork and beef. This hearty dish, typically served with rice, collard greens, and orange slices, is a staple in Rio's food scene. A generous serving of feijoada at a local restaurant usually costs between R$40 and R$80, reflecting its status as both a comfort food and a significant cultural dish.

For seafood enthusiasts, Rio offers the "moqueca," a flavorful fish stew made with coconut milk, tomatoes, onions, and peppers. This dish, often served with rice and a side of farofa (toasted cassava flour), ranges from R$50 to

R$100 depending on the restaurant and portion size. The moqueca exemplifies the region's commitment to using fresh, local ingredients to create dishes that are as vibrant as the city itself.

The capital city of Brasília showcases a different aspect of Brazilian cuisine, emphasizing modern interpretations and upscale dining experiences. Churrascarias, or Brazilian steakhouses, are particularly popular here. These establishments offer an all-you-can-eat experience featuring a variety of grilled meats served tableside. The price for this indulgent experience typically ranges from R$100 to R$200 per person, making it a great choice for those looking to enjoy a substantial meal in a lively, communal atmosphere.

Brasília also boasts a number of fine dining establishments where chefs put a contemporary spin on traditional Brazilian ingredients. At these restaurants, diners might encounter gourmet versions of dishes such as "arroz de pato" (duck rice) or "bobó de camarão" (shrimp in a creamy manioc sauce). Expect to spend between R$150 and R$300 for a full meal, including multiple courses and premium wines, in these high-end venues.

Traveling to the northern regions of Brazil, especially the Amazon, reveals a unique culinary world rooted in indigenous traditions and local ingredients. Amazonian cuisine often features dishes made from rare fruits and vegetables, providing a taste of the rainforest's rich biodiversity. A popular local dish is "tacacá," a tangy soup made with manioc, shrimp, and jambu (an herb that gives a slight numbing sensation). Enjoying a bowl of tacacá typically costs between R$20 and R$40.

Another standout from the Amazon is "pato no tucupi," a duck dish cooked in a vibrant, yellow sauce made from manioc root. This dish offers a distinct flavor profile and is usually priced between R$50 and R$80. The use of local ingredients in these dishes not only supports regional agriculture but also offers travelers an authentic taste of the Amazon.

Beverages in Brazil range from refreshing non-alcoholic options to vibrant cocktails. The caipirinha, Brazil's national cocktail, is a must-try. Made from cachaça (a spirit distilled from sugarcane), lime, and sugar, this cocktail offers a refreshing and slightly tangy flavor. A caipirinha is typically priced between R$20 and R$40 at bars and restaurants. For those preferring non-alcoholic drinks, "guaraná," a soda made from the guaraná berry native to the Amazon, is a popular choice and is available for around R$5 to R$10 per bottle.

To complete a Brazilian culinary experience, don't overlook the diverse array of fresh fruits. Juices and smoothies made from fruits like açaí, cupuaçu, and mango are both delicious and nutritious. An açaí bowl, often topped with granola and fresh fruit, is a popular choice and typically costs between R$20 and R$40. These fruity treats offer a sweet and healthy way to enjoy Brazil's rich agricultural offerings.

The food and drink scene in Brazil is as diverse and dynamic as the country itself. From street food stalls to high-end restaurants, each meal offers a glimpse into the local culture and traditions. Whether indulging in traditional dishes or exploring innovative culinary creations, travelers will find that Brazilian cuisine provides an enriching and memorable part of their journey.

Carnival and Festivals

Carnival and festivals are an integral part of the vibrant tapestry that defines the travel experience in Brazil. These events are not merely gatherings; they are immersive cultural spectacles that showcase the country's rich heritage, dynamic traditions, and unparalleled energy. For travelers, engaging in these celebrations offers a unique glimpse into Brazilian life that goes beyond typical tourist experiences.

Carnival in Rio de Janeiro

The Rio de Janeiro Carnival is arguably the most famous festival in Brazil, attracting millions of visitors from around the globe. Held annually in February or March, this grand celebration is renowned for its extravagant parades, colorful costumes, and samba music. The festivities take place over several days, culminating in a grand parade at the Sambadrome, where samba schools from across the city compete with dazzling floats and choreographed performances. Tickets for the Sambadrome can range from R$200 to R$1,000, depending on the seating area and the day of attendance. For those who wish to experience the street parties, or "blocos," access is generally free, though some may charge a nominal fee for special areas or amenities.

São Paulo Carnival

São Paulo's Carnival is another major event, celebrated with a similar fervor to Rio's. Held in the city's Sambadrome, the São Paulo Carnival showcases the best of local samba schools with a slightly different flavor. The festivities also include a vibrant street party scene that rivals Rio's, with numerous blocos throughout the city. Tickets for the parade in the São Paulo Sambadrome typically range from R$150 to R$800. The street parties offer free access, but special viewing areas or VIP experiences might incur additional costs.

Salvador's Carnival

In Salvador, the Carnival is a unique and electrifying experience known for its massive street parties and the distinctive sound of Axé music. Unlike the parades in Rio or São Paulo, Salvador's Carnival is characterized by its "trios elétricos"—large trucks equipped with sound systems and stages that move through the streets, accompanied by throngs of revelers dancing and singing along. The event generally takes place in February or March, with festivities lasting up to a week. While access to some areas is free, special camarotes (private viewing areas) can range from R$200 to R$1,500, offering a more comfortable vantage point and additional amenities.

Festa Junina

Festa Junina, celebrated in June and July, is a traditional Brazilian festival that honors the harvest season. Known for its folk music, traditional dances, and rustic foods, this festival is deeply rooted in rural customs. Celebrated across Brazil, the Festa Junina features bonfires, square dancing, and hearty dishes such as corn on the cob and sweet treats like pamonha and canjica. In larger cities, themed events and parties might charge entry fees ranging from R$50 to R$200, though many local celebrations are free to attend.

Parintins Folklore Festival

The Parintins Folklore Festival, held annually in June on the island of Parintins in the Amazon, is a vibrant celebration of Amazonian culture and folklore. The festival features a dramatic competition between two folklore groups, Garantido and Caprichoso, who perform elaborate, colorful presentations that recount myths and legends of the region. The festival is a significant cultural event and offers a unique insight into Amazonian traditions. Tickets for the arena events are generally priced between R$100 and R$500.

Oktoberfest in Blumenau

Though its origins are German, the Oktoberfest in Blumenau, held in October, is a significant celebration in Brazil that draws on the country's German heritage. Held in the city of Blumenau, this festival features traditional German music, dance, and cuisine, along with vibrant parades and costume contests. The event spans over two weeks and attracts visitors interested in experiencing a blend of Brazilian and German cultures. Entrance to the festival is typically around

R$30 to R$100, with additional costs for food, beverages, and special events.

Festival de Cachaça

For those interested in Brazil's distinctive spirit, the Festival de Cachaça, held in the town of Paraty, is an excellent choice. Celebrated in July, this festival is dedicated to cachaça, the Brazilian sugarcane liquor, and includes tastings, workshops, and cultural activities related to this iconic drink. The festival attracts cachaça enthusiasts and provides an opportunity to explore Brazilian culinary traditions. Entry fees range from R$50 to R$200, depending on the activities included.

Festival Internacional de Teatro

The Festival Internacional de Teatro in Curitiba is a major cultural event that showcases a diverse range of theatrical performances from around the world. Held in March, the festival features performances from local and international artists, offering a rich cultural experience for theater enthusiasts. Tickets vary widely based on the performance, typically ranging from R$30 to R$150.

In summary, Brazil's carnivals and festivals offer an array of experiences that reflect the country's vibrant cultural diversity. From the world-renowned Carnival in Rio to the festive street parties in Salvador, each event provides a unique window into Brazilian life, making them essential experiences for any traveler looking to immerse themselves in the country's exuberant spirit.

Wildlife and Nature Reserves

Exploring wildlife and nature reserves in Brazil offers a truly immersive experience, catering to travelers with a passion for nature and conservation. This South American gem, renowned for its biodiversity, is home to numerous protected areas that serve as sanctuaries for an astonishing array of flora and fauna. For those seeking an enriching adventure, the following highlights present a glimpse into the wonders that await in Brazil's natural reserves.

1. **Pantanal:** Often referred to as the world's largest tropical wetland, the Pantanal is a mosaic of lakes, rivers, and savannahs stretching across the central-western part of Brazil. It's renowned for its incredible wildlife sightings, including jaguars, capybaras, and caimans. The best time to visit is during the dry season, from May to September, when wildlife congregates around remaining water sources, making them easier to spot. Entrance fees typically range from R$30 to R$70 per person, depending on the

specific lodge or tour operator. Guided tours can range from R$500 to R$1,200 per day, which often include transportation, meals, and expert naturalist guides.

2. **Iguaçu National Park:** This UNESCO World Heritage Site is home to the spectacular Iguaçu Falls, one of the largest and most impressive waterfall systems in the world. The park's lush rainforest is a haven for wildlife such as the jaguar, ocelot, and a plethora of bird species. Visitors can explore the park via well-maintained trails and boardwalks, which provide various vantage points of the falls and the surrounding jungle. Entrance fees are about R$70 to R$100 per person. While the park itself is accessible by public transportation, guided tours typically cost between R$400 and R$800, which can include additional excursions such as boat rides or helicopter tours over the falls.

3. **Amazon Rainforest:** Spanning several countries, Brazil's portion of the Amazon is the heart of the world's largest tropical rainforest. This vast expanse of

greenery is crucial for global biodiversity and climate regulation. The reserve offers unparalleled opportunities to witness exotic wildlife, from the elusive jaguar to colorful macaws and playful river dolphins. The Amazon is best explored through river cruises or jungle lodges, with trips ranging from a few days to several weeks. Entrance fees to various lodges and tours can vary widely, generally from R$200 to R$500 per person per day. Multi-day river cruises and comprehensive guided tours can cost between R$2,000 and R$6,000, depending on the luxury level and inclusions.

4. **Chapada Diamantina National Park:** Located in the state of Bahia, this park is celebrated for its dramatic landscapes, including deep canyons, towering plateaus, and stunning waterfalls. It's a haven for trekkers and outdoor enthusiasts. The park's diverse habitats support a variety of species, including the endangered maned wolf and numerous bird species. Trails such as the Fumaça Falls and the Pati Valley offer breathtaking views and unique wildlife sightings.

The entrance fee is approximately R$30 to R$50 per person. Guided hiking tours typically cost between R$200 and R$500 per day, depending on the length and complexity of the trek.

5. **Serra da Capivara National Park:** This park, located in the state of Piauí, is renowned for its archaeological significance, housing some of the oldest rock art in the Americas. Its semi-arid landscape, dotted with rugged hills and caves, is also a refuge for unique wildlife, including the Brazilian deer and the endangered golden lancehead pit viper. The park's entrance fee is around R$50 to R$70 per person. Guided tours, which offer insights into both the natural and cultural heritage of the area, range from R$300 to R$600 per day.

6. **Lençóis Maranhenses National Park:** Known for its otherworldly landscapes of white sand dunes and crystal-clear lagoons, Lençóis Maranhenses is located in the state of Maranhão. This park is particularly famous for its seasonal lagoons, which form during the rainy season and offer spectacular views and

swimming opportunities. Wildlife in this area includes capuchin monkeys and various bird species. The entrance fee is approximately R$30 to R$50 per person. Tours that include transportation and guided exploration of the dunes typically range from R$200 to R$500.

7. **Reserva Extrativista do Médio Juruá:** Situated in the Amazon Basin, this reserve is managed by local communities who practice sustainable forestry and fishing. It offers a glimpse into traditional Amazonian lifestyles while providing opportunities to see wildlife like the Amazonian manatee and various primates. Entrance fees and tour costs vary significantly depending on the length and type of experience, generally ranging from R$100 to R$400 per day.

Visiting these reserves not only provides a chance to connect deeply with nature but also supports the ongoing conservation efforts crucial to preserving Brazil's rich natural heritage. Travelers are encouraged to respect local guidelines and participate in eco-friendly practices to ensure these pristine environments remain intact for future generations. Each destination offers a unique perspective on Brazil's natural splendor, making them worthwhile stops for any nature enthusiast.

Chapter 4: Practical Information

Safety and Security

As you prepare for your journey to the vibrant land of samba, stunning beaches, and lush rainforests, safety and security are likely top of mind. With some basic precautions and an understanding of the local context, you can minimize risks and maximize your enjoyment of this incredible destination.

Understanding Local Conditions

Like any country, there are areas that are considered safer than others. Major cities like Rio de Janeiro and São Paulo have their share of petty crime, while smaller towns and rural areas tend to be quieter. Being aware of your surroundings and taking necessary precautions can go a long way in ensuring your safety.

Petty Crime and Theft

Petty crime and theft are common concerns for travelers. To protect yourself and your belongings:

1. Be mindful of your belongings, especially in crowded areas and public transportation
2. Avoid carrying large amounts of cash and use reputable exchange services
3. Keep valuables secure and consider using a hotel safe or locker
4. Avoid walking alone in dimly lit or deserted areas, especially at night

Violent Crime

Violent crime is a concern in some areas, particularly in major cities. To minimize risks:

1. Avoid traveling alone at night
2. Use reputable taxi services or ride-sharing apps
3. Avoid displaying signs of wealth (e.g., expensive jewelry or watches)
4. Stay informed about local conditions and avoid areas with high crime rates

Health and Wellness

In addition to physical safety, it's essential to prioritize your health and wellness. Some tips to keep in mind:

1. Consult your doctor before traveling and ensure you have all necessary vaccinations
2. Take necessary precautions against mosquito-borne illnesses like Zika and dengue fever
3. Stay hydrated and bring sunscreen to protect against the sun's strong rays
4. Be aware of local water quality and stick to bottled or filtered water

Natural Disasters

South America is prone to natural disasters, including floods, landslides, and earthquakes. To stay safe:

1. Stay informed about weather conditions and local alerts
2. Follow evacuation orders and instructions from local authorities

3. Stay away from flood-prone areas and avoid traveling during heavy rainfall

Respecting Local Customs and Laws

To avoid any issues during your stay, be sure to respect local customs and laws. Some key considerations:

1. Familiarize yourself with local dress codes and customs, especially when visiting churches or attending cultural events
2. Be aware of local laws and regulations, including those related to drug use and possession
3. Respect the environment and local wildlife, especially in protected areas like national parks

Staying Informed

Finally, staying informed is key to staying safe and secure. Consider the following:

1. Register with your government's travel advisory department to receive important safety and security updates

2. Stay up-to-date with local news and events that may impact your travel plans

3. Follow local authorities and travel experts on social media for real-time advice and insights

Additional Safety Tips

1. Learn some basic Portuguese phrases to communicate with locals

2. Carry a portable charger and keep your phone charged

3. Avoid using ATMs in isolated areas

4. Keep your hotel room door locked and secure

Money and Currency

Currency Considerations for Travelers:

Currency fluctuations and exchange rates can significantly impact your travel experience. As you prepare for your journey to Brazil, understanding the local currency and managing your finances effectively will help ensure an stress-free and enjoyable trip.

Brazil's Official Currency:

The Brazilian Real (R$) is the official currency, subdivided into 100 centavos. You'll find various denominations of banknotes (R$2, R$5, R$10, R$20, R$50, R$100) and coins (R$0.01, R$0.05, R$0.10, R$0.25, R$0.50, R$1).

Exchanging Currency: Options and Tips

To exchange your money, consider the following options:

- Airport currency exchange offices
- Banks
- Currency exchange bureaus

- ATMs (withdrawing local currency)

When exchanging currency:

- Compare rates among different providers
- Avoid exchanging money at airports or hotels (higher fees)
- Use reputable currency exchange services
- Keep some local currency for small purchases

ATMs and Credit Cards in Brazil

Major credit cards (Visa, Mastercard, American Express) are widely accepted in tourist areas. Inform your bank about your travel plans to avoid transaction issues.

- ATM withdrawal fees: R$10-R$30 per transaction
- Credit card transaction fees: 2-5% per transaction

Managing Your Finances in Brazil

To make the most of your money:

- Use credit cards for larger transactions

- Keep cash for small purchases and local transportation
- Monitor exchange rates to optimize your spending
- Avoid carrying large amounts of cash

Tipping and Gratuities in Brazil

Tipping is customary in Brazil:

- Restaurants and bars: 10% of the total bill
- Taxi drivers: R$1-R$2 per ride
- Hotel staff: R$5-R$10 per bag (porters)
- Tour guides: R$20-R$50 per day

Budgeting and Expenses in Brazil

To plan your expenses:

- Accommodation: R$100-R$500 per night
- Meals: R$20-R$50 per meal
- Transportation: R$5-R$20 per ride
- Attractions: R$10-R$50 per person

Additional Financial Tips for Travelers

- Learn some basic Portuguese phrases to communicate with locals
- Carry a portable charger and keep your phone charged
- Avoid using public Wi-Fi for financial transactions
- Keep your hotel room door locked and secure

Government Resources for Travelers

For the latest information on currency regulations and financial guidelines, consult the following government resources:

- U.S. Department of State: Travel Advisory website
- Central Bank of Brazil: Official website
- Brazilian Ministry of Tourism: Official website

Recommended Financial Apps for Travelers

- XE Currency (iOS, Android)
- TransferWise (iOS, Android)
- Google Wallet (iOS, Android)

Recommended Financial Services for Travelers

- Visa Travel Money
- Mastercard Cash Passport
- American Express Travelers Cheques

By understanding Brazil's currency, managing your finances effectively, and staying informed, you'll be well-equipped to navigate the country's financial landscape. Remember to prioritize financial safety, budget accordingly, and enjoy your journey.

Currency Conversion Rates (approximate)

- USD $1 = R$5.00-R$5.55
- EUR €1 = R$5.50-R$6.50
- GBP £1 = R$6.50-R$7.50

Check the latest exchange rates before your trip to ensure accurate information.

Updated Currency Information

As of 2023, Brazil has implemented new regulations to facilitate international transactions:

- Contactless payment methods are widely accepted

- Digital wallets like Apple Pay and Google Pay are available

- ATMs now dispense smaller denominations (R$10, R$20)

Stay informed about the latest developments to ensure a seamless financial experience during your trip.

Communication (Phone, Internet)

Communication is key to navigating any foreign destination, and Brazil is no exception. As you prepare for your journey, understanding the local communication landscape will help ensure an stress-free and enjoyable trip.

Brazil has a comprehensive mobile network, with major operators including:

- Vivo
- Claro
- TIM
- Oi

To stay connected:

1. Purchase a local SIM card (approx. R$10-R$30)
2. Activate international roaming with your home provider
3. Use a prepaid phone plan (approx. R$20-R$50 per month)

Internet Access in Brazil

- Wi-Fi is available in most hotels, restaurants, and cafes

- Internet cafes (lan houses) are common in urban areas

- Mobile data plans offer reliable connectivity

Staying Connected with Family and Friends

To keep loved ones informed about your travels:

- Use messaging apps like WhatsApp, Facebook Messenger, or Skype

- Make voice calls with VoIP services like Viber or Google Voice

- Send regular email updates

Language Barriers and Translation Tools

While Portuguese is the official language, many Brazilians speak some English, especially in tourist areas. To overcome language barriers:

- Learn basic Portuguese phrases (e.g., "obrigado" for "thank you")
- Use translation apps like Google Translate or iTranslate
- Carry a phrasebook or dictionary

Social Media and Online Platforms

Stay connected with locals and fellow travelers through:

- Social media platforms (Facebook, Instagram, Twitter)
- Online forums and travel communities (e.g., Reddit's r/Brazil)
- Travel blogs and websites

Safety and Security Considerations

To protect your communication devices:

- Use secure Wi-Fi networks and VPNs
- Keep devices password-protected
- Be cautious of public Wi-Fi and avoid sensitive transactions

Additional Tips for Travelers

- Purchase a portable power bank for extra battery life
- Consider a waterproof phone case for outdoor activities
- Download essential apps before arrival (e.g., maps, language translators)

Recommended Communication Apps

- WhatsApp (iOS, Android)
- Skype (iOS, Android)
- Google Translate (iOS, Android)
- Viber (iOS, Android)

Recommended Prepaid Phone Plans

- Vivo's Prepaid Plan (approx. R$20-R$50 per month)
- Claro's Prepaid Plan (approx. R$20-R$50 per month)
- TIM's Prepaid Plan (approx. R$20-R$50 per month)

Effective communication is vital to navigating Brazil's vibrant culture and stunning landscapes. By staying connected, overcoming language barriers, and prioritizing safety, you'll be well-equipped to make the most of your journey.

Communication Costs (approximate)

- Local SIM card: R$10-R$30
- Prepaid phone plan: R$20-R$50 per month
- Mobile data plan: R$10-R$30 per GB

Useful Portuguese Phrases

- Obrigado (thank you)
- Por favor (please)
- Desculpe (excuse me)
- Sim/Não (yes/no)

Stay connected, stay informed, and enjoy your Brazilian adventure!

Language and Etiquette

Language is a key element to understanding any culture, and when visiting Brazil, it's important to recognize that Portuguese, not Spanish, is the official language. This is a common misconception among travelers due to Brazil's location in Latin America. Portuguese is spoken by nearly the entire population, and though some Brazilians in tourist-heavy areas might speak English or Spanish, the majority of people communicate solely in their native tongue. Learning a few basic Portuguese phrases will go a long way in facilitating smoother interactions, enhancing your travel experience, and showing respect for the local culture.

Portuguese Language Basics

While many Brazilians speak some English, learning basic Portuguese phrases will go a long way:

- Hello: Olá (OH-lah)
- Thank you: Obrigado (oh-bree-GAH-doo) / Obrigada (oh-bree-GAH-dah)

- Please: Por favor (pohr fah-VOHR)
- Yes/No: Sim/Não (SEEM/NAH-oh)
- Excuse me: Desculpe (deh-SKOOL-peh)

Pronunciation Tips

- Pay attention to accents and vowel pronunciation
- Practice pronunciation before arrival
- Download language learning apps like Duolingo or Babbel

Non-Verbal Communication

Brazilians are known for their warmth, and non-verbal communication is just as important as spoken language. Body language is expressive, and people often stand close to one another during conversations, which is a sign of friendliness rather than intrusiveness.

- Physical touch is common among friends and acquaintances
- Direct eye contact shows respect and interest
- Use open and approachable body language

Etiquette Essentials

- Greet people with a handshake or kiss on the cheek
- Use formal titles (Senhor/Senhora) until invited to use first names
- Respect for elders and tradition is deeply rooted in Brazilian culture

Table Manners

- Wait for the host to indicate where to sit
- Keep hands visible on the table
- Try a little of everything on your plate

Social Etiquette

- Be prepared for lively conversations and debates
- Show interest in others' lives and families
- Avoid discussing politics or sensitive topics

Regional Variations

- Be aware of regional differences in language and customs
- Learn local expressions and traditions

Additional Tips for Travelers

- Learn key phrases in indigenous languages (e.g., Tupi)
- Respect local customs and traditions
- Be patient and open-minded when communicating

Recommended Language Learning Resources

- Duolingo (iOS, Android)
- Babbel (iOS, Android)
- PortuguesePod101 (podcast)

Recommended Cultural Immersion Programs

- Homestay programs with local families
- Language exchange programs with locals
- Cultural workshops and festivals

Language Learning Apps (approximate costs)

- Duolingo: free
- Babbel: $12.95/month
- PortuguesePod101: $4/month

Transportation (Flights, Buses, Taxis)

Transportation in Brazil offers a variety of options for travelers, from domestic flights connecting major cities to extensive bus networks that serve both urban and rural areas. Navigating these systems effectively can enhance your travel experience, whether you're exploring the country's vibrant cities or heading into more remote regions.

Flights: Connecting Cities Across Brazil

Given the vast size of Brazil, flying is often the most convenient way to cover long distances. Major airlines such as LATAM, Gol, and Azul operate extensive domestic routes, connecting cities like Rio de Janeiro, São Paulo, Brasília, Salvador, and others. If you're traveling from Rio de Janeiro to São Paulo, for instance, a flight takes just over an hour, while the same journey by car or bus could take six to eight hours.

Prices for domestic flights vary based on the season, how far in advance you book, and the airline. For a one-way flight from Rio de Janeiro to São Paulo, you can expect to pay between R$200 and R$600, depending on demand. Prices for flights to more remote areas, such as the Amazon region, can be higher, sometimes ranging from R$800 to R$1,500. To get the best deals, it's advisable to book early, especially if you're traveling during high season or during festivals like Carnival.

Buses: The Affordable Way to Explore

Buses are one of the most popular and affordable ways to travel across Brazil, especially for short to medium distances. Brazil's bus system is extensive and reliable, connecting major cities as well as smaller towns. Long-distance buses, known as "ônibus rodoviários," are generally comfortable and offer different service classes. These include standard seats, semi-reclining, and fully reclining seats, which are perfect for overnight journeys.

For example, a trip from Rio de Janeiro to São Paulo by bus takes about six hours, and ticket prices range from R$100 to R$180, depending on the class of service. Buses from Rio to destinations like Belo Horizonte or Paraty might cost between R$90 and R$150. Many bus companies, such as

Expresso do Sul, Itapemirim, and Cometa, offer online booking, making it easier to plan your journey.

When traveling by bus, it's advisable to book your tickets in advance, especially during holiday seasons when routes can fill up quickly. The terminals, or "rodoviárias," in major cities are typically large and can be busy, so arriving early ensures you have time to navigate them and find your bus.

Taxis and Ride-Sharing: Convenient City Travel

For city travel, taxis are readily available in most urban areas, and ride-sharing apps like Uber and 99 are popular alternatives. Both options offer convenience, especially when traveling at night or in areas where public transport may be less reliable. Taxis in Brazil are generally safe, and most have meters, but it's still a good idea to check that the meter is running when you get in.

In major cities like Rio de Janeiro and São Paulo, short taxi rides typically start at around R$6 to R$8, with a per-kilometer charge of about R$2 to R$3. For example, a taxi ride from Copacabana to the Christ the Redeemer statue in Rio may cost between R$50 and R$80, depending on traffic.

Ride-sharing apps often offer lower fares compared to traditional taxis. A 20-minute Uber ride in São Paulo might cost around R$20 to R$40, depending on the time of day and demand. Ride-sharing apps also provide the benefit of being able to track your route, see your fare in advance, and pay digitally, adding an extra layer of convenience and safety.

Public Transportation

Brazil's major cities also have public transportation systems, including buses, trams, and metro lines. São Paulo and Rio de Janeiro have well-developed metro systems, with fares around R$5 per trip. These systems are often the fastest way to get around during peak traffic hours, especially in congested areas.

While buses are more common in smaller cities, they can be crowded and sometimes difficult to navigate due to the lack of English signage. However, apps like Google Maps and Moovit can help you track routes and timetables, making public transport a viable option for budget-conscious travelers.

Useful Transportation Terms

- Aeroporto (ah-ee-ROH-poh-too): airport
- Ônibus (OH-nee-boos): bus
- Táxi (TAH-see): taxi
- Aluguel de carro (ah-LOO-ghee-ool deh KA-roh): car rental

Shopping and Souvenirs

Shopping in Brazil is an experience that combines vibrant culture, stunning beauty, and exceptional value. As you explore this incredible country, you'll discover a wide range of unique souvenirs, local handicrafts, and delicious treats to remind you of your journey.

Must-Visit Shopping Destinations

1. Rio de Janeiro's Hippie Fair (Feira Hippie): Sundays, Ipanema Beach
   - Handmade crafts, jewelry, and clothing: R$20-R$100 (approx. $5-$25 USD)
2. São Paulo's Municipal Market (Mercado Municipal): daily, São Paulo
   - Fresh produce, meats, and local specialties: R$10-R$30 (approx. $2.50-$7.50 USD)
3. Salvador's Afro-Brazilian Market (Mercado Afro-Brasileiro): daily, Salvador
   - African-inspired handicrafts and textiles: R$20-R$50 (approx. $5-$12.50 USD)

4. Iguatemi São Paulo: daily, São Paulo

    -   Luxury shopping mall with international brands: R$50-R$500 (approx. $12.50-$125 USD)

Unique Souvenirs

1. Handmade handicrafts: R$20-R$100 (approx. $5-$25 USD)

    -   Woodcarvings, pottery, and woven baskets

2. Local specialties: R$10-R$50 (approx. $2.50-$12.50 USD)

    -   -Coffee, cachaça, chocolates, and tropical fruits

3. Colorful clothing and accessories: R$20-R$100 (approx. $5-$25 USD)

    -   Scarves, hats, and vibrant textiles

4. Brazilian gemstones: R$50-R$500 (approx. $12.50-$125 USD)

    -   Emeralds, rubies, and sapphires

Tips for Smart Shopping

1. Bargain and negotiate prices, especially at markets
2. Inspect products carefully before purchasing

3. Use reputable currency exchange services

4. Keep valuables secure and be mindful of pickpocketing

Local Markets and Fairs

1. Rio de Janeiro's Copacabana Night Market: Fridays and Saturdays
   - Street food, live music, and local handicrafts

2. São Paulo's Liberdade Neighborhood: daily
   - Japanese and Asian-inspired shopping and cuisine

3. Salvador's Old Town: daily
   - Historic architecture, local markets, and Afro-Brazilian culture

Recommended Shopping Apps

1. ShopSãoPaulo (iOS, Android)

2. RioShopping (iOS, Android)

3. BrazilHandmade (iOS, Android)

Prices (approximate)

- Handmade handicrafts: R$20-R$100 (approx. $5-$25 USD)
- Local specialties: R$10-R$50 (approx. $2.50-$12.50 USD)
- Colorful clothing and accessories: R$20-R$100 (approx. $5-$25 USD)
- Brazilian gemstones: R$50-R$500 (approx. $12.50-$125 USD)

Useful Shopping Terms

- Mercado (mehr-KAH-doo): market
- Loja (LOH-zhah): store
- Preço (preh-SOH): price
- Barganhar (bar-gah-NYAR): to bargain

Chapter 5: Regional Guides

North Brazil (Manaus, Belém)

North Brazil, home to Manaus and Belém, offers travelers a unique blend of natural wonder, rich culture, and historical significance. As the gateway to the Amazon Rainforest, this region captivates adventurers, nature lovers, and cultural explorers alike. For those visiting Brazil, the northern part of the country provides an opportunity to experience the untouched beauty of the Amazon, bustling river cities, and a rich blend of indigenous and Portuguese influences. Whether you're trekking through dense forests, exploring vibrant markets, or enjoying local cuisine, North Brazil promises an unforgettable journey.

Manaus

Manaus, the capital of Amazonas state, is the heart of the Amazon Rainforest. Situated on the banks of the Rio Negro, this city is often the starting point for most Amazonian adventures. Its location is both geographically and culturally significant, acting as a hub for trade, culture, and tourism within the rainforest.

Getting There

Most travelers reach Manaus by plane, with regular flights from major Brazilian cities like São Paulo and Rio de Janeiro. Manaus International Airport (Eduardo Gomes International Airport) is well connected to the rest of the country and also offers a few international flights. Upon arrival, travelers are greeted by the humid, tropical climate and lush surroundings that define this region.

What to Do in Manaus

1. Exploring the Amazon Rainforest: A visit to Manaus isn't complete without a venture into the Amazon Rainforest. Many tour operators offer river cruises, guided hikes, and eco-lodge stays where you can experience the incredible biodiversity of the region. You'll likely encounter unique wildlife like pink river dolphins, jaguars, macaws, and countless other species. Additionally, guided tours offer a chance to meet indigenous communities who have lived in harmony with the forest for centuries, giving you an insight into their traditions and way of life.

2. Meeting of the Waters: One of Manaus' most famous attractions is the "Meeting of the Waters," where the dark waters of the Rio Negro meet the sandy-colored waters of the Rio Solimões. Due to differences in temperature, speed, and density, these rivers run side by side without mixing for several kilometers. It's an awe-inspiring sight and a great opportunity for riverboat tours or even fishing excursions.

3. Teatro Amazonas (Amazon Theatre): Manaus' history as a center of the rubber boom in the late 19th century is reflected in the grand architecture of the city. The most iconic building is the Teatro Amazonas, an opulent opera house built in 1896. This beautifully restored theater offers guided tours, as well as performances that range from classical to modern genres. The building itself is a marvel, with its Renaissance-style design, imported European materials, and a dome covered in 36,000 colored ceramic tiles, representing the Brazilian national flag.

4. Mercado Municipal Adolpho Lisboa: For a taste of local life, the Mercado Municipal Adolpho Lisboa is a must-visit. This market, inspired by the Les Halles market in Paris, offers everything from fresh fish and exotic fruits to handcrafted goods. It's a sensory overload and a great place to sample Amazonian delicacies like tucumã, cupuaçu, and pirarucu, or to pick up souvenirs such as traditional crafts made by indigenous artisans.

Best Time to Visit

Manaus has a tropical rainforest climate, with temperatures averaging around 25-30°C year-round. The best time to visit is during the dry season from June to November, when river levels are lower, making trekking and wildlife spotting easier. However, even the rainy season (December to May) can be a good time for river-based activities, as the water levels rise and create opportunities for exploring flooded forests by canoe.

Belém:

Belém, the capital of Pará state, is located at the mouth of the Amazon River, making it an essential stop for travelers who want to experience the natural and cultural beauty of North Brazil. Known for its colonial architecture, bustling markets, and access to the Amazon Delta, Belém offers a distinct charm that differs from the more urbanized regions of Brazil.

Getting There

Like Manaus, Belém is accessible by air, with Val de Cans International Airport serving as the primary gateway. Flights connect Belém to other major Brazilian cities, as well as some international destinations. Visitors can also arrive via boat, as Belém's port is a hub for river travel in the Amazon basin.

What to Do in Belém

1. Ver-o-Peso Market: One of the oldest and largest markets in Brazil, Ver-o-Peso is the heartbeat of Belém. Established in the 17th century, it serves as a marketplace for regional produce, seafood, spices, medicinal herbs, and handmade crafts. Wandering through its stalls, you'll encounter the exotic ingredients that define Amazonian cuisine, such as açaí, Brazil nuts, jambu, and manioc flour. It's an immersive experience, offering a true glimpse into the daily life and culture of the people of Pará.

2. Forte do Castelo: For history enthusiasts, the Forte do Castelo, built in the early 17th century, provides insight into Belém's colonial past. This fortress, located near the riverfront, was originally constructed by the Portuguese to defend against Dutch invaders. Today, it offers panoramic views of the city and the river, as well as a small museum with exhibits on the history of the region.

3. Mangal das Garças: Located on the banks of the Guamá River, Mangal das Garças is a unique park and ecological reserve that showcases the diverse flora and fauna of the Amazon. Visitors can explore its aviary, butterfly house, and orchid garden, or climb the observation tower for sweeping views of the surrounding area. It's a peaceful escape from the hustle and bustle of the city and an opportunity to learn about the region's ecosystems.

4. Ilha de Marajó: For those looking for a true off-the-beaten-path experience, a visit to Ilha de Marajó is a must. Located at the mouth of the Amazon River, this massive island is famous for its water buffalo, traditional Marajoara pottery, and pristine beaches. Marajó offers a unique combination of rainforest, savannah, and wetlands, providing ample opportunities for bird watching, horseback riding, and exploring remote fishing villages.

Best Time to Visit

Belém enjoys a tropical rainforest climate with high humidity and temperatures ranging between 25-32°C. The dry season from July to November is the ideal time to visit, as rainfall is less frequent and the weather is more conducive to exploring the city's outdoor attractions.

Final Thoughts

North Brazil, with Manaus and Belém as its crown jewels, offers travelers an unparalleled opportunity to experience the Amazon in all its glory. From exploring the world's largest rainforest to wandering through vibrant markets, this region is a blend of natural wonders and cultural treasures. Whether you're seeking adventure in the wild or a deeper understanding of Brazil's rich history, North Brazil delivers a once-in-a-lifetime experience that should be on every traveler's itinerary.

Northeast Brazil (Recife, Olinda)

Northeast Brazil is a land of contrasts, where rich history and vibrant culture meet tropical beaches and dynamic urban landscapes. Two cities that embody this unique blend are Recife and Olinda. Located in the state of Pernambuco, these cities are among the most captivating destinations in the region, offering travelers a chance to experience Brazil's cultural heritage, breathtaking scenery, and lively social scene. Whether you're an adventurer, a history buff, or simply in search of relaxation, a trip to Recife and Olinda is sure to leave a lasting impression.

Recife:

Known as the "Venice of Brazil," Recife is a coastal city distinguished by its intricate network of rivers, canals, and bridges that crisscross the city. Its name is derived from the Portuguese word for "reef," as Recife's shoreline is protected by coral reefs that form natural barriers against the Atlantic Ocean. For travelers, Recife is an excellent starting point for discovering the vibrant culture and natural beauty of Northeast Brazil.

Historical Highlights

Recife's historical center is a treasure trove of colonial-era architecture and cultural landmarks. The neighborhood of Recife Antigo is where the city's history comes alive. Once the heart of colonial Recife, this area is now a lively district filled with restored 17th and 18th-century buildings, museums, art galleries, and lively bars.

One must-visit location is the Kahal Zur Israel Synagogue, the first synagogue established in the Americas, dating back to the 1630s when Recife was briefly under Dutch rule. Another landmark is the Paço do Frevo, a cultural center dedicated to the preservation of frevo music and dance, a UNESCO-recognized intangible cultural heritage that is native to Recife. The annual Carnival of Recife is famous for its frenetic rhythms of frevo and maracatu music, drawing both locals and tourists to the streets in a colorful explosion of music and dance.

If you're a fan of history, the Instituto Ricardo Brennand is a must-see. This sprawling museum complex is home to an impressive collection of European and Brazilian art, weaponry, and artifacts, set within a picturesque, castle-like structure surrounded by gardens.

Beaches and Natural Beauty

While Recife is a bustling urban center, it also boasts some beautiful beaches that are perfect for relaxation or water sports. The city's coastline is lined with palm trees, and the coral reefs that gave Recife its name also create calm, lagoon-like waters in certain areas, making it ideal for swimming.

Boa Viagem Beach, located in the southern part of Recife, is the most famous and accessible beach in the city. It stretches for over 7 kilometers (4.3 miles) and offers clear, warm waters, white sand, and a variety of beachside restaurants serving fresh seafood. While the beach is generally safe for swimming during low tide, caution is advised due to the presence of sharks in deeper waters.

For those seeking nature beyond the city's beaches, the nearby island of Itamaracá and the Coroa do Avião sandbar are great options for a day trip. Itamaracá is known for its historical Fort Orange and offers opportunities for kayaking, snorkeling, and exploring mangrove forests.

Olinda:

Just a short drive from Recife, the historic city of Olinda is one of Brazil's best-preserved colonial towns and a UNESCO World Heritage site. Perched on a series of hills overlooking the Atlantic Ocean, Olinda offers stunning views, cobblestone streets, and a wealth of beautifully preserved churches, convents, and colorful colonial houses. Olinda has long been a haven for artists and musicians, and its bohemian spirit is palpable in the city's galleries, workshops, and lively festivals.

Architectural Marvels

One of Olinda's main attractions is its wealth of Baroque architecture, much of which dates back to the 16th and 17th centuries. The city's many churches are particularly noteworthy, with the São Bento Monastery being a standout. Its gilded altar is one of the most intricate examples of Baroque art in Brazil, and the monastery also houses a collection of sacred art.

Another must-see is the Convent of São Francisco, which is the oldest Franciscan convent in Brazil. The convent's interior is decorated with Portuguese tile work, and the adjacent Church of Nossa Senhora das Neves features stunning wood carvings and gold leaf ornamentation.

Carnival in Olinda

While Recife's Carnival is famous for its massive street parades and energetic atmosphere, Olinda's Carnival is more intimate and laid-back, offering visitors the chance to experience Brazil's most famous festival in a more traditional setting. During Carnival, Olinda's narrow streets come alive with giant puppets known as Bonecos Gigantes, costumed revelers, and spontaneous music performances. Unlike Rio de Janeiro's more commercialized Carnival, Olinda's celebrations remain rooted in local culture, featuring traditional frevo music and maracatu performances.

Even outside of Carnival season, Olinda's cultural scene is lively. The city is home to numerous art studios, and visitors can often watch local artists at work. If you're lucky, you might stumble upon a samba de roda or an afro-Brazilian drumming circle, which frequently pop up in the city's public squares.

Dining and Nightlife

The culinary scene in Recife and Olinda offers a rich array of local flavors, particularly seafood. Recife is home to a number of top-notch restaurants where travelers can sample traditional dishes such as moqueca (a seafood stew made with coconut milk), carne de sol (sun-dried beef), and bolo de rolo (a rolled cake with guava filling).

For a more local dining experience, visit the Mercado da Madalena or the Casa de Banhos, where you can try regional specialties like tapioca, acarajé, and caldinho (a small cup of broth, usually made with shrimp or beans).

After sunset, the vibrant nightlife of Recife Antigo comes to life. Its bars and nightclubs host a variety of live music performances, including samba, frevo, and forró, a traditional northeastern Brazilian music style.

Practical Information

Recife is easily accessible via Guararapes International Airport, which serves domestic and international flights. From there, Olinda is just a 20-minute drive away. The climate in this region is tropical, with warm temperatures year-round and a rainy season from April to July. The best time to visit is during the dry season, particularly in February or March if you're hoping to experience Carnival.

Public transportation in Recife is fairly extensive, with buses and metro lines serving the main areas. However, for greater flexibility and convenience, many travelers opt to rent a car or use ride-hailing services to get around the city and surrounding areas.

Southeast Brazil (Rio, São Paulo)

Southeast Brazil is a region that effortlessly balances the past and present, showcasing an energetic blend of modernity and rich history. As one of the most visited areas in Latin America, Southeast Brazil encompasses some of the country's most iconic cities, including Rio de Janeiro and São Paulo, each offering its own distinct character and myriad attractions. For travelers embarking on a journey to this region, the opportunities to explore cultural, historical, and natural wonders are seemingly endless. Whether you're drawn to Rio's breathtaking beaches or São Paulo's thriving art scene, Southeast Brazil promises an unforgettable experience.

Rio de Janeiro:

Known as the "Cidade Maravilhosa" or Marvelous City, Rio de Janeiro is an iconic destination that has long captivated travelers with its stunning landscapes, lively cultural scene, and exuberant festivities. Nestled between dramatic mountains and the Atlantic Ocean, Rio is famous for its world-renowned beaches, such as Copacabana and Ipanema, where golden sands meet the vibrant rhythms of Brazilian life.

One of Rio's most famous landmarks is the Christ the Redeemer statue, perched atop Corcovado Mountain. Standing at 98 feet tall, this colossal statue is not only a symbol of Christianity but also an emblem of Brazilian hospitality. The views from the summit of Corcovado provide a panoramic sweep of the city's beaches, forests, and urban sprawl. Another unmissable landmark is Sugarloaf Mountain, accessible via a scenic cable car ride. From the top, visitors are treated to an awe-inspiring view of the city's bays and harbors, a favorite spot for sunset enthusiasts.

For a deeper dive into Brazilian culture, travelers should experience Samba in its birthplace, the Lapa neighborhood. Lapa is the center of Rio's nightlife, with its famous arches and historical bars where live samba music fills the air. If visiting during Carnival, expect the streets of Rio to burst into life with flamboyant costumes, parades, and street parties, known as "blocos," drawing millions from across the world.

Beyond the city's urban allure, Rio is also home to Tijuca National Park, the largest urban rainforest in the world. Hiking through Tijuca is a must for nature lovers, where waterfalls, caves, and diverse flora and fauna offer a respite from the bustling city. This balance between urban vibrancy and natural beauty is part of what makes Rio a unique travel destination.

São Paulo:

São Paulo, the largest city in Brazil and the Southern Hemisphere, is a global metropolis that rivals the world's leading cities in culture, finance, and gastronomy. Unlike Rio's easygoing beach vibe, São Paulo pulses with the energy of a sprawling urban giant where over 12 million residents coexist in a melting pot of cultures. The city is a hub for international business and creative arts, making it an essential destination for travelers seeking a more cosmopolitan experience.

The city's art scene is particularly renowned, with a wealth of galleries and museums that showcase both local and international talent. The São Paulo Museum of Art (MASP) is a standout, not only for its collection, which includes works from the Renaissance to contemporary Brazilian art, but also for its striking modernist architecture. Nearby, Ibirapuera Park provides a green oasis in the heart of the city, home to the Museum of Modern Art and several cultural institutions. Designed by the legendary architect Oscar Niemeyer, this park is a perfect place to enjoy art, nature, and leisure in one setting.

São Paulo is also Brazil's culinary capital, and its food scene reflects the city's diverse cultural makeup. From Michelin-starred restaurants like D.O.M., helmed by chef Alex Atala, to the vast array of Japanese cuisine in the Liberdade neighborhood, which houses the largest Japanese community outside of Japan, São Paulo is a gastronomic delight. Mercado Municipal, the city's sprawling market, is a must-visit for food enthusiasts eager to sample local delicacies like mortadella sandwiches, tropical fruits, and freshly made pastéis.

Shopping in São Paulo is a major attraction for fashion lovers. The city is known for its high-end shopping districts like

Jardins, where international luxury brands are complemented by local Brazilian designers. Alternatively, visitors can explore the bohemian neighborhood of Vila Madalena, known for its vibrant street art and independent boutiques.

How to Navigate Between Rio and São Paulo

Traveling between Rio de Janeiro and São Paulo is both convenient and scenic. The two cities are separated by approximately 430 kilometers (267 miles), and the most popular modes of travel include flights, buses, or private car journeys. Flights between the cities take just over an hour, with several daily connections offered by Brazil's major airlines, such as Gol and LATAM. For travelers looking to enjoy the picturesque countryside, taking a bus is a comfortable and economical option, with journey times of around six hours. The roads between Rio and São Paulo pass through beautiful coastal and mountainous landscapes, offering scenic stops along the way.

Unique Experiences Beyond the Cities

While Rio and São Paulo are the primary draws for international travelers, Southeast Brazil offers many other unique experiences worth exploring. For a taste of Brazil's colonial history, a visit to Paraty is a must. This charming coastal town, halfway between Rio and São Paulo, boasts well-preserved 18th-century architecture and is a UNESCO World Heritage site. Paraty is also known for its pristine beaches and islands, perfect for those seeking a peaceful retreat from the hustle and bustle of the larger cities.

For nature lovers, the Serra da Mantiqueira mountain range offers numerous hiking trails, waterfalls, and mountain resorts. The region's cooler climate and lush landscapes make it an ideal getaway for eco-tourism. Towns like Campos do Jordão are popular during the winter months, attracting visitors with their alpine-style chalets and cool weather festivals.

Additionally, Southeast Brazil is home to one of the country's most important cultural festivals, the Festa de Nossa Senhora Aparecida, held annually in the city of Aparecida.

This religious festival, honoring Brazil's patron saint, attracts millions of pilgrims and is a deeply moving experience for those interested in spiritual tourism.

South Brazil (Curitiba, Porto Alegre)

South Brazil, an often overlooked gem in the vast landscape of the country, offers a rich and unique experience for travelers. This region, encompassing cities like Curitiba and Porto Alegre, boasts a blend of natural beauty, cultural heritage, and vibrant urban life that provides a refreshing contrast to the more commonly visited destinations in Brazil.

Curitiba: A City of Innovation and Nature

Curitiba, the capital of Paraná state, is renowned for its innovative urban planning and green spaces. The city has earned acclaim for its effective public transportation system, which includes an extensive network of bus rapid transit lanes. This system, implemented in the 1970s, remains a model for cities worldwide, demonstrating Curitiba's commitment to sustainable development and efficient urban living.

A key highlight of Curitiba is its commitment to environmental preservation. The city is home to numerous parks and green spaces, including the Botanical Garden of

Curitiba. This expansive garden features a stunning glass greenhouse that houses a diverse collection of plants from the Atlantic Forest biome. The park also offers walking trails and lakes, making it a perfect spot for relaxation and a closer look at the region's flora.

Another notable attraction in Curitiba is the Ópera de Arame, or Wire Opera House, an architectural marvel constructed from steel and glass. This unique venue hosts a variety of performances, from classical music to contemporary theater. The surrounding park, which includes a picturesque lake and a forest, enhances the experience of visiting this cultural landmark.

Curitiba's historic neighborhoods also offer intriguing exploration opportunities. The Santa Felicidade district is renowned for its Italian heritage and is a culinary hotspot, with numerous restaurants serving traditional Italian dishes. The district's vibrant atmosphere and rich history make it a must-visit for food enthusiasts and those interested in the city's cultural influences.

Porto Alegre: A Cultural and Economic Hub

Moving south to Porto Alegre, the capital of Rio Grande do Sul, travelers will find a city brimming with cultural richness and economic vitality. Porto Alegre is a significant economic center, with a diverse industrial base and a thriving port, which plays a crucial role in the region's trade and commerce.

One of the city's defining features is its dynamic cultural scene. The Fundacao Ibere Camargo, an impressive modern art museum located on the banks of the Guaíba River, is a focal point for contemporary art enthusiasts. The museum's striking architecture, characterized by its undulating forms and extensive use of glass, complements the innovative art it houses. Exhibitions at the museum frequently showcase both Brazilian and international artists, providing a diverse range of artistic experiences.

The city's vibrant nightlife and culinary scene are also noteworthy. Porto Alegre boasts a variety of bars, restaurants, and live music venues, catering to a range of tastes and preferences. The city's culinary offerings are heavily influenced by the gaucho tradition, featuring robust flavors and dishes such as churrasco, a type of barbecue that reflects the region's meat-loving culture.

For those interested in exploring the local culture, the Mercado Público is an essential visit. This historic market, established in the late 19th century, offers an array of local products, from fresh produce to artisanal goods. It serves as a lively gathering place where visitors can experience the city's everyday life and taste local delicacies.

Natural Wonders and Outdoor Activities

Both Curitiba and Porto Alegre offer access to stunning natural landscapes that enhance the region's appeal. Near Curitiba, the Serra do Mar mountain range provides opportunities for hiking and outdoor adventure. The region is home to several protected areas and national parks, such as the Parque Nacional de São Joaquim, which features rugged terrain, waterfalls, and diverse wildlife.

Porto Alegre is similarly well-positioned for those who enjoy outdoor activities. The nearby Lagoa dos Patos, one of the largest lagoons in South America, offers scenic views and opportunities for birdwatching. The surrounding region includes numerous trails and natural reserves where visitors can immerse themselves in the local flora and fauna.

Cultural Experiences and Local Events

South Brazil's cultural landscape is enriched by a variety of local festivals and events that reflect the region's diverse heritage. Curitiba hosts the Festival de Teatro, one of the largest theater festivals in Brazil, attracting artists and audiences from across the globe. This event highlights the city's commitment to the arts and its role as a cultural hub.

Porto Alegre also offers a range of cultural events throughout the year, including the Porto Alegre em Cena, an international theater festival that features performances from around the world. Additionally, the city celebrates its rich gaucho heritage with traditional festivals such as the Festa do Peão, which includes rodeo events, folk music, and dance.

Central West Brazil (Brasília, Goiânia)

Central West Brazil, a region distinguished by its vibrant culture, dynamic cities, and breathtaking natural landscapes, offers an array of experiences for travelers seeking a unique Brazilian adventure. This area, encompassing the federal capital Brasília and the bustling city of Goiânia, serves as a gateway to exploring the heartland of Brazil, where the pulse of the nation's growth and tradition converge.

Brasília, the capital city, is renowned for its modernist architecture and urban planning. Designed by the Brazilian architect Oscar Niemeyer and the urban planner Lúcio Costa, Brasília was officially inaugurated in 1960 with the intention of promoting development in the interior of Brazil. The city's layout, in the shape of an airplane, and its futuristic buildings make it a fascinating destination for architecture enthusiasts. Key landmarks include the Palácio da Alvorada, the official residence of the President, and the Catedral Metropolitana, known for its striking crown-like structure and impressive stained glass.

Brasília is also a cultural hub, with several museums and cultural institutions. The Museu Nacional, or National Museum, offers extensive exhibits on Brazilian history and culture, while the Centro Cultural Banco do Brasil (CCBB) frequently hosts art exhibitions, theater performances, and film screenings. For those interested in political history, the Congresso Nacional provides guided tours that delve into the workings of Brazil's government and its legislative processes.

In contrast to Brasília's modernity, Goiânia presents a more relaxed, yet vibrant atmosphere. Established in 1933, Goiânia is known for its green spaces and leisurely pace. The city is recognized for its commitment to preserving nature, as evidenced by its numerous parks and tree-lined streets. The Flamboyant Park, one of the largest urban parks in Brazil, offers a serene escape with its walking trails, picnic areas, and artificial lake. The city's urban planning reflects a harmonious balance between development and green spaces, making it an attractive destination for both residents and visitors.

Goiânia is also a cultural and gastronomic hotspot. The city hosts various cultural events throughout the year, including music festivals, art fairs, and traditional Brazilian celebrations. The local cuisine is a highlight, featuring traditional dishes such as pequi rice and pamonha (corn-based dishes), which offer a taste of the region's culinary heritage. The Feira da Lua, a popular night market, is a must-visit for those looking to experience local food, crafts, and live music.

The Central West region is not only defined by its cities but also by its natural wonders. The nearby Chapada dos Veadeiros National Park is a notable destination for nature enthusiasts. This park, a UNESCO World Heritage site, is renowned for its striking landscapes, including waterfalls, canyons, and expansive plateaus. The park's diverse ecosystems provide opportunities for hiking, birdwatching, and exploring unique geological formations. The Alto Paraíso de Goiás, a small town near the park, serves as a gateway for exploring these natural wonders and offers accommodations and services for visitors.

In addition to Chapada dos Veadeiros, the Pantanal, one of the world's largest tropical wetlands, extends into the Central West region. This ecologically significant area is teeming with wildlife, including jaguars, capybaras, and an array of bird species. The Pantanal offers exceptional opportunities for eco-tourism, with guided tours that provide insight into the region's biodiversity and conservation efforts. Boat tours, jeep safaris, and guided nature walks are popular ways to experience the Pantanal's rich wildlife and stunning landscapes.

Central West Brazil also benefits from its central location, making it an accessible starting point for exploring other parts of the country. The region's transportation infrastructure, including Brasília's major international airport, facilitates travel to other Brazilian destinations. Whether journeying to the Amazon rainforest, the beaches of the northeast, or the southern wine regions, travelers can easily continue their exploration from this central hub.

For those interested in local culture and history, the region offers various opportunities for immersion. Traditional festivals and events often reflect the region's diverse cultural influences, from indigenous traditions to Afro-Brazilian heritage. Participating in these festivals provides deeper insights into the local way of life and the vibrant traditions that shape the Central West.

Travelers to Central West Brazil will find that this region offers a rich blend of modern urban experiences, cultural immersion, and natural beauty. With its distinctive cities like Brasília and Goiânia, along with its impressive natural landscapes such as the Chapada dos Veadeiros and the Pantanal, Central West Brazil promises a compelling and multifaceted adventure. Whether exploring architectural marvels, indulging in local cuisine, or immersing oneself in nature, visitors are sure to leave with lasting memories and a deeper appreciation for the heart of Brazil.

Conclusion

Glossary of Brazilian Terms

1. Olá

Translation: Hello

Usage: This is a universal greeting in Brazil, appropriate for any situation, whether you're meeting someone for the first time or greeting friends.

2. Obrigado / Obrigada

Translation: Thank you

Usage: "Obrigado" is used by men, and "obrigada" is used by women. It's polite to use this expression when someone has done something for you or provided assistance.

3. Por favor

Translation: Please

Usage: This term is used when requesting something politely. For example, "Pode me ajudar, por favor?" means "Can you help me, please?"

4. Desculpe / Desculpa

Translation: Sorry

Usage: Use "desculpe" or "desculpa" to apologize for mistakes or inconveniences. It's always good to use this when you've accidentally bumped into someone or made a minor error.

5. Sim / Não

Translation: Yes / No

Usage: These basic terms are essential for answering questions or expressing agreement or disagreement.

6. Onde fica...?

Translation: Where is...?

Usage: Use this phrase to ask for directions. For example, "Onde fica o banheiro?" means "Where is the bathroom?"

7. Quanto custa?

Translation: How much does it cost?

Usage: This question is helpful when shopping or dining out. For instance, if you want to know the price of a meal, ask, "Quanto custa este prato?"

8. Dinheiro / Cartão de crédito

Translation: Cash / Credit card

Usage: Knowing these terms will help you handle payments. "Dinheiro" refers to cash, while "cartão de crédito" refers to a credit card.

9. Água

Translation: Water

Usage: A basic term you'll need to request water at restaurants or when you're thirsty. You might say, "Por favor, um copo de água."

10. Comida / Prato

Translation: Food / Dish

Usage: "Comida" is a general term for food, while "prato" refers to a specific dish. For example, "Qual é o prato do dia?" means "What is the dish of the day?"

11. Restaurante

Translation: Restaurant

Usage: Use this term to refer to places where you can eat. If you need a place to dine, you might ask, "Você conhece um bom restaurante por aqui?"

12. Hospedagem / Hotel

Translation: Accommodation / Hotel

Usage: "Hospedagem" is a broader term for accommodation, and "hotel" specifically refers to hotels. You can ask, "Onde está o hotel mais próximo?" to find the nearest hotel.

13. Transporte

Translation: Transportation

Usage: This term covers all forms of transport. When you need information on getting around, you can inquire, "Qual é o melhor transporte para chegar ao centro?"

14. Segurança

Translation: Safety

Usage: Important to know, especially in tourist areas. You might ask, "Esta área é segura?" to find out if a location is safe.

15. A conta, por favor

Translation: The bill, please

Usage: When you're ready to pay at a restaurant, use this phrase to ask for your bill.

16. Rua / Avenida

Translation: Street / Avenue

Usage: "Rua" refers to streets, while "avenida" refers to avenues. These terms are useful when asking for directions. For instance, "Qual é a rua onde fica o museu?"

17. Mercado

Translation: Market

Usage: Use this term to refer to places where you can buy fresh produce and other goods. You might ask, "Onde fica o mercado mais próximo?"

18. Farmácia

Translation: Pharmacy

Usage: This is where you go for medications or health supplies. If you need to find one, ask, "Tem uma farmácia perto daqui?"

19. Polícia

Translation: Police

Usage: Knowing this term can be crucial in case of emergencies. You might need to ask, "Onde está a delegacia de polícia?"

20. Ajuda

Translation: Help

Usage: Use this term when you need assistance. For example, "Preciso de ajuda" means "I need help."

21. Prazer

Translation: Pleasure / Nice to meet you

Usage: When meeting someone for the first time, you can say, "Prazer em conhecê-lo," which means "Nice to meet you."

22. Festa / Carnaval

Translation: Party / Carnival

Usage: Brazil is famous for its celebrations, with "festa" being a general term for parties and "Carnaval" referring to the famous festival held before Lent.

23. Praia

Translation: Beach

Usage: Essential for a country with such beautiful coastlines. Ask, "Qual é a melhor praia para visitar?" to find out the best beaches.

24. Guia turístico

Translation: Tour guide

Usage: If you need assistance exploring, a "guia turístico" can provide valuable insights and information about various attractions.

25. Mapa

Translation: Map

Usage: Helpful for navigation, ask for a "mapa" if you need directions or want to explore the area.

26. Souvenir

Translation: Souvenir

Usage: When shopping for mementos, you can use this term to ask about souvenirs. For example, "Onde posso comprar um souvenir?"

27. Informação

Translation: Information

Usage: This term is useful when seeking details. You might ask, "Onde posso encontrar mais informações sobre os pontos turísticos?"

Familiarizing yourself with these terms will make your travels in Brazil smoother and more enjoyable. Engaging with locals and understanding the language enhances your travel experience and helps you make lasting memories in this beautiful country.

Useful Contacts and Resources

Embassies and Consulates

- U.S. Embassy in Brasília: +55 61 3312-7000
- U.K. Embassy in Brasília: +55 61 3329-2300
- Canadian Embassy in Brasília: +55 61 3424-5400

Government Agencies

- Brazilian Ministry of Tourism: +55 61 2023-8000
- Brazilian National Immigration Agency: +55 61 2023-7000
- Brazilian Federal Police: +55 61 2023-6000

Tourist Information Centers

- Rio de Janeiro: +55 21 2541-7522
- São Paulo: +55 11 2226-0400
- Salvador: +55 71 3321-2463

Health and Medical Services

- Brazilian Ministry of Health: +55 61 2023-8000

- SOS Médico (Emergency Medical Service): +55 11 3145-0500

Travel Apps

- Brazil Travel Assistant (iOS, Android)
- Rio de Janeiro Guide (iOS, Android)
- São Paulo Travel Guide (iOS, Android)

Transportation

- Brazilian National Transportation Agency: +55 61 2023-7000
- Rio de Janeiro Metro: +55 21 2240-2414
- São Paulo Metro: +55 11 3331-7777

Accommodation

- Brazilian Hotel Association: +55 61 2023-8000
- (link unavailable) (Brazil): +55 11 3958-5800
- Airbnb (Brazil): +55 11 3958-5800

Safety and Security

- Brazilian Federal Police: +55 61 2023-6000

- Rio de Janeiro Police: +55 21 2332-2924
- São Paulo Police: +55 11 3321-5000

Language and Translation

- Google Translate (Brazilian Portuguese): +55 11 3958-5800
- Brazilian Portuguese Language Courses: +55 61 2023-8000

Additional Resources

- Brazilian Ministry of Foreign Affairs: Official website
- Brazilian National Tourism Board: Official website
- World Health Organization (Brazil): Official website

Brazilian Holidays and Events

Here is a comprehensive list of holidays and events in Brazil:

Fixed Holidays

1. New Year's Day (January 1st)
2. Good Friday (variable date)
3. Easter Sunday (variable date)
4. Tiradentes Day (April 21st)
5. Labor Day (May 1st)
6. Independence Day (September 7th)
7. Our Lady of Aparecida Day (October 12th)
8. All Souls' Day (November 2nd)
9. Republic Proclamation Day (November 15th)
10. Christmas Day (December 25th)

Variable Holidays

1. Carnaval (5 days before Ash Wednesday)
2. Ash Wednesday (46 days before Easter Sunday)
3. Holy Week (variable date)
4. Easter Week (variable date)

5. Corpus Christi (60 days after Easter Sunday)

6. Festa do Divino Espírito Santo (50 days after Easter Sunday)

7. Festa de São João (June 24th)

8. Festa de São Pedro (June 29th)

9. Festa de São Paulo (January 25th)

Events

1. Rio de Janeiro International Film Festival (September)

2. São Paulo Art Biennial (October)

3. Salvador Carnival (February/March)

4. Rio de Janeiro Carnival (February/March)

5. Festa do Peão de Boiadeiro (August)

6. Festa de Iemanjá (February 2nd)

7. Festa de Oxóssi (February 3rd)

8. Festa de Xangô (February 4th)

9. Festa de São Jorge (April 23rd)

10. Festa de Nossa Senhora da Conceição (December 8th)

Regional Events

1. Festa do Boi-Bumbá (June, Pará state)

2. Festa de São Sebastião (January, Rio de Janeiro state)

3. Festa de Nossa Senhora dos Navegantes (February, Bahia state)

4. Festa de São José (March, Pernambuco state)

5. Festa de Nossa Senhora da Abadia (April, Minas Gerais state)

Note: This list is not exhaustive, and dates may vary from year to year.

Printed in Great Britain
by Amazon

47977843R00106